PRIVATE OWNER WAGONS
A SECOND COLLECTION

compiled by
KEITH TURTON

British Library Cataloguing-in-Publication Data. A catalogue record for this book is available from the British Library
ISBN 1 899889 14 0

Lightmoor Press
120 Farmers Close, Witney, Oxfordshire, OX28 1NR
Printed by Cromwell Press, Trowbridge

Lightmoor Press

PRIVATE OWNER WAGONS
A SECOND COLLECTION

Dated 16th August 1915 this view, at a so far unidentified location, shows workers of Ellis & Everard with their delivery horse, coal dray and a couple of wagons being unloaded. Ellis & Everard were a wide spread merchant through Leicestershire and surrounding counties.

Taken at Port Talbot in the late 1920s, the wagons are mainly from anthracite producers and await their shipping appointments. Those in the background are from the Vale of Neath Colliery Company's Aberpergwm Colliery and the nearby Ynisarwed Colliery at Resolven – the prominent interloper being the Gueret, Llewellyn & Merrett wagon, which may have been loaded at the Crynant Colliery near Neath. In the foreground are wagons from William Perch in three different lettering schemes, the left-most with PERCH LTD on the diagonal and two from RIGOS Colliery; one each from Gwaunclawdd and Aberpergwm; and one from the rlatively short-lived Welsh Anthracite, the latter of especial interest as it names the collieries which it has already subsumed. These include Abercrave and International, both featured in *Private Owner Wagons: A First Collection*, which were subsequently jettisoned by Welsh Anthracite to a rival company but ended up in an inevitable fate called Amalgamated Anthracite.

Great Western Collection, NRM

CONTENTS

Taken in the autumn of 1929 at Penarth Docks, Cardiff, this scene is typical of the Bristol Channel ports from Newport to Llanelly, where siding space for over 55,000 wagons was provided as train after train of Welsh coal arrived for export, to be transferred to ships holds or bunkers at coal loaders such as the hydraulic hoists illustrated. There are at least 200 wagons in this scene, and like the traffic from most Welsh collieries, those of a single company arrived by the trainload, empty returns often had to be sorted before being sent back up the valleys for reloading. The two nearest sidings show empty wagons for the Ocean, Cambrian and Glamorgan collieries. The next rake loaded with large steam coal belong to D. Davis & Sons Ferndale Collieries of Maerdy and include a number from H. G. Lewis of Cardiff which would have been on hire. These include those lettered with the large HGL and those with the small script in the top left-hand corner. Behind and partly obscured are wagons belonging to Stephenson Clarke. Nearest the docks are wagons of Cory Bros and the final row is a mixture of Albion Colliery, Nixons Navigation and D. Davis and Son, all three of which would, within a year, be part of Welsh Associated Collieries Ltd.   *GWR Collection, NRM*

INTRODUCTION

WHY a Second Collection to follow a First Collection? Simply, this is a reference to what kept the Private Owner wagon as near as possible to the forefront of my mind in all the years I spent in Australia. Here I accumulated a big collection of well over a thousand ready-to-run, transfers, and kit-built models in 00 gauge of the wagons I had come to love in my early childhood, and not an inch of track to run them on!

Unfortunately, I lived far away from the Hunter Valley of New South Wales, where the British principal was carried on for long after the last wooden bodied unbraked wagon departed from the rails of the opposite side of the world but where I visited as often as possible. That steam traction lasted in that immediate area longer than anywhere else in eastern Australia is probably more than a co-incidence. What was less of a co-incidence was that the region of the Hunter Valley where the clanking of buffers and three link couplings was to be heard was fast becoming one of the premium wine producing regions of the world and embarking on a massive expansion, where acres of grapevines rubbed shoulders with the familiar waste from coal mines with names that evoked memories of Durham and the mining villages of the Welsh Valleys.

The term 'Private Owner Wagon' may eventually become part of the folklore, the legend and the lexicon of the railway history of Britain. It may not reach the status of worship as has the Gresley Pacific, the Somerset & Dorset or the Settle & Carlisle. But the avalanche of new releases of models in 00 gauge in 2003 is a fair indication that its remembrance is not only alive but expanding.

Perhaps it should be made clear at this point that such a description is erroneous, 'Private Operator Wagon' would be far more accurate, for the majority of the wagons described herein, and indeed in the preceding volume and that which is currently in preparation to follow this one, were in fact privately operated by those whose names were emblazoned on their bodies, whereas the true owners –□wagon hire and wagon finance companies –□claimed their ownership by means of metal plates attached to either the underframe or the bodywork. Nevertheless, the legend is indelibly written into the history of our railways and, erroneous or not, it is not likely to be corrected.

Whereas the entire twentieth century produced only thirteen books about the Private Owner wagon, the situation is now being redressed, for it is known that at least three others are in the pipeline, and more are believed to be planned. That there is still material untouched by researchers is obvious from the contents of this volume, which includes a further selection from many parts of the country, the contents again being determined by the availability of photographs and text to match. Historical research into a completely untouched field is exciting enough but the discovery of photographs of wagons by such little known builders as Percival of Chester and Bell of Finningley is a considerable incentive to keep on searching. What amplifies the descriptions that accompany some of the wagons featured herein is that a little bit of extra research, at times in the most unlikely places, changes a brief description of a wagon and its owner to a record of transportation history.

In *A First Collection* coverage was concentrated in particular geographical areas. Ideally, all regions would be covered equally but again this reverts to the lack of photographs and matching data in which The South Coast, East Anglia and Lincolnshire are typical examples: much of Lancashire has been covered by Mr A. J. Watts in his wonderful book *Private Owner Wagons of the Ince Waggon and Iron Works*. Luckily some readers have loaned or donated photographs which have been used herein, and these are acknowledged with much gratitude.

The Welsh collieries and coal merchants were a major force in the trade, something like 20% of the wagons in the country were domiciled in a small area extending through South Wales from Newport to Llanelly and in the mining valleys that reached inland. Little was published in *A First Collection* but some attempt has been made to redress this situation, for it was possible for the author to spend the time necessary in those parts of Wales where surviving records are held. The Welsh collieries, with their varied spelling, their frequent changes of ownership, lack of longevity and duplicated names, were by far the most challenging and took more time to untangle, but this made it possible to appreciate the metamorphosis which overtook the ownership of the Welsh coal industry over a very short timespan. The outcome is being prepared for the further volumes in this series. As an indication of the complicated nature of the resulting megaliths of the trade, the final composition of Amalgamated Anthracite consisted of what survived from the acquisition of forty different and once independent colliery companies. This included the acquisition of over 12,000 wagons, all of which were re-branded as many as four times.

Such a transformation of the ownership of the coal industry occurred outside of the memories of most of us today, but it was repeated in the brewing trade in the 1970s and 1980s which many of us will remember with heavy hearts, for many names, almost immortal bastions of traditional English ale, were swallowed up by outsiders whose only object of worship was the cash register. Here any comparison must end, for what was produced by the Welsh mines was consistent with the quality before both corporate mergers and nationalisation. Whether the coal ran out or the demand for coal of its quality ran out first may never be truthfully answered, but in the end the nationalised industry would consider any excuse to shut down a mine even if it was profitable and there were reserves untouched, for to the end the quality never declined. In contrast, what came out of the breweries did. Thankfully, some of the more enlightened resisted the enticement of the balance sheet and still thrived. That legendary names in the South Wales coalfield, such as Norths Navigation, Nixons Navigation, Lewis Merthyr and Duffryn Aberdare, disappeared in the 1930s without a whimper, all that was destroyed were the coal owners' names. In complete contrast, fifty years later, much loved names with traditions dating back centuries such as Trumans, Threlfalls, Greens, Hammonds, Duttons and Charringtons disappeared into global conglomerates despite much protest. With them disappeared some of the heart of England. Concurrently so did workplaces of equally legendary status such as Denaby, Bolsover, Llanbradach, Sherwood and Grimethorpe, the latter immortalised globally in the film 'Brassed Off'.

The subject of wagon utilisation, touched on briefly in *A First Collection* is revived by a second study of the minutes of the City of Birmingham Gas Department when referring to the several meetings between its executive and Sir Josiah Stamp, Chairman of the LMS.

The genesis of a wagon can be described in several phases:

(A) An order is placed by a consumer for a number of wagons with a manufacturer.

(B) This order is then placed on the factory: type, dimensions, capacity and door arrangements are determined. If the wagon owner has submitted a design and colour, this is specified on the works order and followed by the manufacturer's paint shop. In most instances the maker is given the responsibility of designing the layout of the wagon lettering, although in some cases a similar style is used by several builders suggesting a degree of influence from the owner to use his 'house style'.

(C) The completed wagon is inspected by an official of the railway company with which it is to be registered or an agent for them, and if satisfactory, is approved for service, and a numbered registration plate affixed to the underframe.

(D) Details of the registration are entered into the Private Owner Wagon Register book of that railway, showing owner, builder, delivery date, and, if not owned outright, financier. The latter is indicated by a plate affixed to the wagon underframe or on its end. Some registers showed the dimensions of the wagon also.

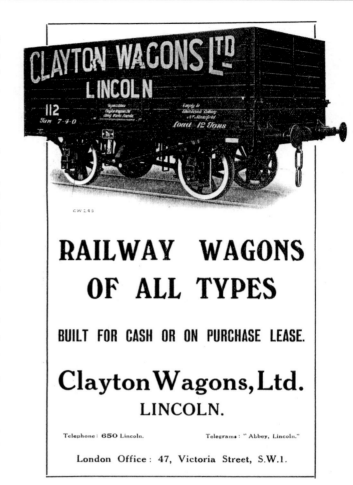

The registration plate was the equivalent of the indelible identification of a car today, and in theory was supposedly carried on that wagon for its entire existence. If the wagon changed hands, i.e. was sold off during a routine fleet updating, theoretically this was reported to the company with which the wagon was registered and the alteration duly recorded in the Wagon Register, but this was not always carried out (or if it was, the information was not passed on to the keepers of the Wagon Register books) and many wagons changed hands without being recorded. Similarly, when a wagon was broken up the registration details were supposedly passed on to whichever company it was registered with, to be recorded in the Wagon Register. In actual fact this was carried out only intermittently and therefore the disposal of a large majority of wagons was never recorded. In similar vein, if a wagon changed hands as a result of a merger or absorption of a company, this usually went unrecorded.

Many wagons were actually purchased or owned by hiring or finance companies who often owned fleets many times the size of that of a large colliery, for example the Gloucester company owned over 8,000, the short lived and controversial Cardiff firm of H. G. Lewis owned and rented out over 24,000 and had fingers in the affairs of many more, the Yorkshire Wagon Co. also rented out around 25,000. The livery in which these wagons ran was rarely, if ever, recorded, although there are photographs in this volume of some H. G. Lewis wagons. Those which were hired out for a reasonable period, usually a year or longer, may have been lettered with the operator's name and

address in small letters at the top left-hand corner, although some received a full livery which rendered them almost indistinguishable from new. Trading of secondhand wagons between hire companies was reasonably common, even when under rental, and the purchase of such wagons by collieries and large and financially sound users, was far more widespread than one would think.

The alphabetical format has been retained, as has the policy of identifying wagon colours, surely the most contentious, debated, and least recorded aspect of Private Owner wagon study:

(A) If the body colour is known for certain, it is stated as such.

(B) If the body colour is not known, it is also stated as such.

(C) If the body colour is gleaned from a source which cannot be confirmed, it is stated as 'appears to be' or an anecdotal source is quoted.

(D) All body measurements are amended to the nearest inch. In many instances no body measurements are quoted as they were not recorded, either by the makers or in the Wagon Registers, and only the Gloucester company consistently identified its wagons, but only new wagons, with their dimensions. The Midland Railway, with its usual efficiency, recorded all body dimensions and considerably more data in its registers.

Once again, some of the photographs featured herein have been reproduced before, with and without additional details. It should be made clear that any wagon or owner featured that has been the subject of a previous publication is included as further evidence of that wagon or owner has come to light. This is not a reflection on the original author and should never be looked upon as such. As the credits in the appropriate place in this volume will show, records are scattered at archival institutions all over the country and further deposits at some of the less likely ones in recent times have added considerably to our knowledge, those discovered at Rotherham are of substantial importance and have been drawn on heavily. Likewise and unexpectedly, those at the Merseyside Maritime Museum were also of great interest.

In the previous volume, it was stated that the most common body colour was undoubtedly red. Reading this particular volume, one might be persuaded to think that black was the most common wagon colour, as many Welsh collieries – whose wagons where overwhelmingly painted black – are featured. For some reason the collieries of Yorkshire, Notts, Derbyshire, Staffordshire, Leicestershire and Warwickshire favoured red wagons, with grey running a poor third and all other colours a long way behind.

My own indoctrination into the Private Owner wagon scene when I was very young was at a coalyard, and I have detailed some of its operations from my personal memory bank and that of several veteran coalmen, some now well into their eighties, who, bribed with a pint of their favourite ale, provided an endless stream of humorous anecdotes, some of which have already

been published and a further selection is presented, including a couple where the author was the victim of their leg-pulling. Inevitably, some of the stories they told are unprintable.

Records of the Metropolitan Railway were used to enhance two photographs which were rare in that the wagons depicted were registered with that railway.

In *A First Collection* the variety of wagon owners ranged from 'the biggest municipal owned utility in the country to the landlord of a village pub'. In *A Second Collection* over sixty owners are depicted, these include owners such as Stevens of Oxford where the lack of trading information is offset by a superb collection of photographs showing the development of a wagon fleet over fifty years and the variations in lettering which at times makes modelling a nightmare. Two colliery companies in Wales, Glyncorrwg and Duffryn Rhondda, are amply represented photographically as their chequered history can be described both in text and images. There are one or two photographs which are sub standard, but they are the only photographic record of the wagons of their particular owners, and they have been included specifically for their importance.

To consistently standardise on the presentation and cover price of this series, some fifty owners and feature chapters have been held over to present later in 2004 A Third Collection which will feature more help for modellers, an extended description of the composition of wagon colours, the financial side of wagon ownership, the colliery taken over by the Government in

Inside the paint shop of the Charles Roberts works at Wakefield, several hoppers for Richard Thomas of Scunthorpe are in the process of being painted and lettered. These were part of an order for 135 20-ton and 250 22-tonners built by Roberts between 1936 and 1938, presumably the taller wagons being those of larger capacity. One wonders why the presence of the bowler hat, and if the present day occupational health and safety regulations would tolerate the precarious working positions on the trestles. *Wakefield Collection*

wartime as a prelude to nationalisation, at least one of the Welsh giants, wagon liveries gleaned from the surviving records of Wagon Repairs Limited, and how one of our former colonies copied the British system and where it lasted a lot longer than it did in this country.

To conclude, it has indeed been gratifying to receive so much correspondence and support from established and respected railway authors in this country, as well as a fair amount of good-natured needling from my friends in Australia, where over thirty years ago my first book was published. As with *A First Collection*, the list of acknowledgements is a formidable one and is made with considerable gratitude. In my opening remarks about the inspiration to produce *A First Collection* I confessed to certain aspects of the subject to which my knowledge was not equal to that of others. In this subject the paucity of accurate sources inevitably ends up in errors, as one noted historian told me 'there has never been a book on railway history yet that has not had an error in it.' The author can only write from what information is at hand, and it has been found that there are errors in the records of not only wagon builders, but also owners,

sources that one would think were a paragon of accuracy. I am grateful to those who pointed out those in *A First Collection* and these are acknowledged elsewhere.

An exception which may be considered churlish is that it has to be placed on record that photographs which were eminently suitable for this volume were not considered due to the unreasonable and outrageous demands of their custodians. That the original copyright has long since expired and that in many instances the original photographers are not known does not warrant a substantial payment for their reproduction. It is unfortunate that this has to be placed on record, as some were most co-operative during my research and were aware that it was a historical document and in the general manner of such was not a fictional best seller. Those rare photographs which have never been dusted off for decades deserve better.

Keith Turton,
Ashby-de-la-Zouch,
Leics.
January 2004

In contrast to the Welsh dock scenes at the start of the Introduction is another 'sea of coal' waiting for shipping in hundreds of wagons but this time at Birkenhead Docks in 1910. Wagons of Richardson and McWilliam of Liverpool; Dutton Massey & Co., also of Liverpool; Sneyd Colliery at Burslem; Stirrup & Pye of Stoke-on-Trent; T. B. Grant (location unknown); and Foxfield Colliery, Dilhorne, Staffs; are amongst those whose identity can be determined. *NRM*

The wagon illustrated was supplied secondhand by Gloucester Railway Carriage & Wagon Co. Ltd and bears a paint date of October 1933. It was a seven-plank side and end door vehicle and it will be noted that even as late as 1933 wagons were still being sold with a single set of brakes only, which may explain the tare weight which is unusually low for such a wagon. The livery was black with plain white letters. The italic lettering above the wagon number reads: '*Empty to Treeton Colliery, Rother Vale Collieries, L.M.S. Rly.*'. The solebar carries an interesting selection of plates. The registration plate appears to carry the date 1911 and might have been with the GWR. There are then two old Gloucester **G** plates, the right-hand one being an owner's plate, and a freshly painted example. Finally a Wagon Repairs Ltd mushroom-shaped plate.   *GRC&WCo.*

C. H. ATKINSON Ltd

THE registered office of the company was West Africa House, 25 Water Street, Liverpool. It appears to be a comparative latecomer to the coal distribution scene in Liverpool, as the first directory entry is 1937, when it was listed as 'Colliery Agents and Coal Exporters', although the sales records of the Wath Main Colliery suggest that it was in business back in 1931. In either field it did not challenge the dominance of the large and long established Liverpool coal dealers, such as Dutton Massey, Daniel Rea, Richardson & McWilliam, J. McKelvie, J. P. Higginson, Lancashire Associated Collieries, John Heaton, James Beswick, Montagu Higginson, J. Parkinson and Cory Bros.

The wagon illustrated at the top of the page emptied to the Treeton Colliery of the United Steel Corporation near Rotherham, possibly to load gas coal, whilst that below was empty to Main Colliery, Wigan. Apart from these and the Wath Main Colliery to the north of Barnsley, there are no further records to

A wagon supplied to C. H. Atkinson as photographed at Gloucester in January 1935. It appears to have been supplied secondhand and may not have been built by Gloucester but possibly by Hurst Nelson. The small italic lettering on the left reads: '*Empty to Main Colliery Sidings, Springs Branch, Wigan, L.M.S. Wigan Coal Corporation, Ltd.*' The livery appears to be red with white lettering, shaded black.   *GRC&WCo.*

suggest where Atkinson obtained supplies. This of course depended on the requirements of their clientele, but the trade with Wath Main suggests that high quality steam coal was also sold. This, in the 1930s was in considerable decline in

the shipping trade due to the retirement or conversion of many coal burning ships, and it may have been destined for industry.

MODELS : None

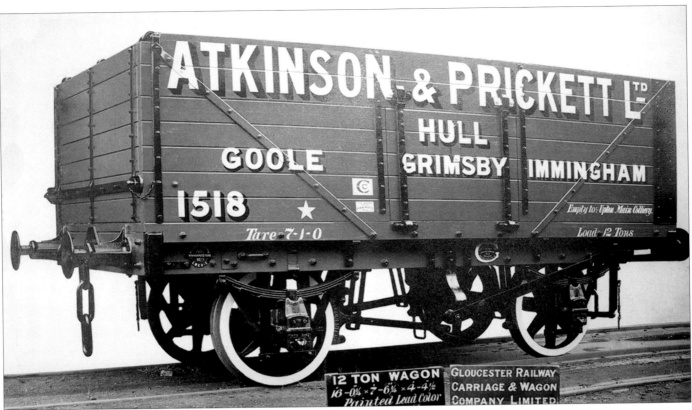

Fleet number 1518 is one of ten wagons delivered in 1935 by the Gloucester company. It has side and end doors and measures internally 16ft 0in. x 7ft 6in. x 4ft 4in. It was painted 'lead colour' with white letters shaded black and black vertical ironwork. Italic lettering at bottom right reads *'Empty to Upton Main Colliery'*. Registered by the LNER, No 8311.   *GRC&WCo.*

No. 1526 was an eight-plank side and end door wagon built concurrently by Charles Roberts Ltd. Assuming that the lettering layout was supplied by the customer, it is interesting to see how the two wagon works interpreted their instructions. The main difference is the word 'Ltd' on the top line, but there are also differences in the size and placement of the rest of the lettering. On the Roberts wagon, all ironwork was black whilst the body is assumed to be grey with white letters shaded back. Small letters at bottom right read 'EMPTY TO MALTBY MAIN COLLIERY.' Again registered by the LNER with the number 8504.   *courtesy HMRS, AAS418*

ATKINSON & PRICKETT Ltd

WITH the fascinating postal address of Land of Green Ginger, Hull, the company was a long established one with varying interests which include the importing and distribution of pit props from Scandinavia, the supply of coal to the fishing fleet and to their own coal burning trading ships as well as local coal supplies.

Offices were located at Hull, Goole, Immingham and Grimsby and the company was trading with the Bullcroft Colliery near Doncaster as early as 1912. In the 1930s coal purchases were recorded from Wath Main, Upton, Welbeck and Bentinck collieries in Notts and Yorkshire but the principal source of supplies is understood to have been the Maltby Main Colliery to the east of Rotherham.

Despite an apparently large wagon fleet, most of the supplies from Bentinck and Welbeck were transported in colliery or railway owned wagons. During the miners strike of 1926 the reverse was in place as Atkinson & Prickett imported coal from Europe to supply local customers as well as the fishing fleet. At this date the company name was 'Atkinson & Prickett Wagon Co. Ltd' but by 1933 had become simply 'Atkinson & Prickett Ltd'.

In 1932 the company commenced hiring wagons from the Gloucester company, twenty wagons being obtained in December of that year and constantly renewed until 1939. New wagons were purchased in 1935 from Gloucester, Roberts, Lancashire & Yorkshire Wagon Co. and Butterley, the latter being all steel 12-ton capacity typical of that manufacturer's standard design. These are detailed below and were all registered with the LNER.

DATE	NUMBERS	BUILDER	REGISTRATION
08.1935	1501 to 1505	L&Y Wagon Co.	7898 to 7902
06.1935	1506 to 1515	S. J. Claye	8269 to 8278
07.1935	1516 to 1525	Gloucester	8509 to 8518
07.1935	1526 to 1530	Charles Roberts	8504 to 8508
05-06.1936	1601 to 1605	Butterley	9531 to 9535
04-07.1937	1606 to 1655	Butterley	10527 to 10576

A single 13-ton all-wooden mineral wagon numbered 1042 was built in January 1943 by A. Gibson Ltd., Hull and registered by LNE-E. Presumably it replaced a condemned wagon. The Company was allowed to return to Butterley for two further small batches of their patent steel wagons:-

Five 14-ton all-steel patent mineral wagons numbered 1701-1705 were built by Butterley in 1943. A further fifteen of similar design but able to carry 16-ton, were built in 1944 and numbered 1706-1719. All were registered by the LNE, the first batch with numbers 611-5 and the second 616-29 .

A sketch of wagon 184 appears in Book 1 of *The Modeller's Sketchbook of Private Owner Wagons* by A. G. Thomas where the lettering layout is very similar to the Gloucester-built example opposite with the livery being given as 'medium grey' with white lettering shaded black.

The company also advertised (in 1912) the ownership of a fleet of steamships and their coal purchases would not only be for customers but also for their own ship's bunkers. As they were large scale suppliers of pit props from Scandinavian countries, and a lot of Yorkshire coal was shipped to Scandinavia via Hull, they could have been exporting it also, their ships being laden in both directions. The range of their wagons would have been limited to traffic from the seaports as indicated on the wagon sides to the collieries of Yorkshire and the Mansfield/ Worksop area of Notts for coal supplies and for the sale of pit props, with possible journeys to the remainder of the Notts/ Derbyshire coalfield and even into Lancashire. Once again, it is the lack of records which are a handicap to a more definite knowledge of their distribution.

In 1957 Atkinson & Prickett Ltd was acquired by Thomas Kettlewell of Hull and still trades today handling bulk liquids and grain.

MODELS : None

The third wagon, No. 1602, is from the first batch built by Butterley. Although the registration date is March 1936, the paint date on the underframe reads '6/36'. The wagon appears to be painted with a dark grey body and white letters shaded black. The panel at the bottom right incorporates the label clip and reads 'Empty to Maltby Main Colliery'.
courtesy HMRS, AAX003

The 12-ton side and end door wagon No. 63 was one of an order for 360 placed with the Gloucester company on May 6th 1912 and registered with the GWR. It has brakes both sides and commode handles at the door end. Also to be noted is that the diagonal bracing has been picked out in black – unusual among wagons from this builder. The wagon has internal dimensions of 15ft 0in. x 7ft 4in. x 4ft 2in. and was painted 'lead' colour with plain white letters and all ironwork was black. Italics in bottom left-hand corner read: 'Empty to Bedwas, Brecon & Merthyr Railway.'. Note the wagon number and tare repeated on the end door. *GRC&WCo.*

BEDWAS NAVIGATION COLLIERY Co. Ltd
BRITISH BENZOL & COAL DISTILLATION Ltd

THE colliery was located at Bedwas, on the Brecon and Merthyr Railway between Trethomas and Bedwas and its more recent trading name was the Bedwas Navigation Colliery Company (1921) Limited. It was owned by one of the most respected names in the Welsh coal industry, the Instones, with its registered office at 52 Leadenhall Street, London. The Instones also had a controlling interest in the Askern Main Colliery near Doncaster. Also at the colliery was a large coking plant employing 35 Becker coke ovens built by Woodall Duckham with a capacity of 200,000 tons of coke a year, as well as the usual by-products. This, according to the wagon sides, was owned by the British Benzol & Coal Distillation Ltd, with S. Instone & Co. Ltd acting as sales agents. The same company also owned a similar plant at the Crigglestone Colliery in Yorkshire. The colliery itself was a large one, producing an annual average of half a million tons of steam and gas coal, rising to 650,000 tons in 1938.

The distribution of Bedwas coal is unknown, but being of such high quality it would have found a ready market for export, bunkering and heavy industry. The Instone family also owned the Instone Transport and Trading Company and the Rumney

No. 331 is a very large convertible 20-ton coke wagon from an order for 200 placed with the Gloucester company in 1929. It is of nine planks (note the very narrow plank second from top) with two doors on each side, each with two door stops, bottom doors and an end door. It is most unusual for the Gloucester company not to declare the wagon livery, instead a comprehensive set of dimensions has been provided: length over buffers 24ft 6in.; length over headstocks 21ft 6in.; inside dimensions: 21ft 0in. x 7ft 6in.; wheelbase 12ft 0in.; height: without coke rails 9ft 3in., with coke rails 11ft 0in.; tare weight without coke rails: 9t. 14cwt 2q., with 9t. 19cwt 3q. The wagons were finished with a red body, unshaded white letters, vertical ironwork black. Italic lettering at bottom right reads: '*Empty to Bedwas Colliery Sidings, Bedwas, G.W.R.*'.

GRC&WCo.

The tank wagon, No. 14, is another Gloucester product and is from an order for five placed in May 1930 and delivered in the following September. The tank is fitted with heating coils and was therefore most probably used for tar. The wagon has the following dimensions: Length over headstocks 17ft 6in.; tank barrel (I.D.) 17ft 4in. x 6ft 3in. diameter; height from rail level to top of screw down valve 11ft 5in.; wheelbase 9ft 0in. As with most tank wagons built by Gloucester painting details are absent from the boards therefore it is difficult to give a body colour. Letters plain white. Rectangular plate on underframe reads 'BRITISH BENZOL AND COAL DISTILLATION LTD, BEDWAS, MON. NO. 14'. Small lettering on the wagon body at left reads '*Empty to* BEDWAS COLLIERY SIDINGS, BEDWAS, G.W.R.' and on right '*Sales Agents-* S. INSTONE & Cᴼ Lᵀᴰ'. Registration was with the GWR, the number being 207.

GRC&WCo.

This view is taken from a booklet produced to commemorate the construction of the Becker coke oven plant for British Benzol. Here there were thirty-five Becker ovens constructed by Woodall-Duckham of London. The associated by-products recovery plant produced, amongst other things, sulphate of ammonia, motor spirit, and tar. Notable in the foreground of the photograph are many Bedwas wagons including two 20-ton all steel, No's 045 and 030, and, in the second siding several of the wooden 20-ton coke wagons – the fourth wagon in with both of its side doors propped-up in the open position. Three wagons further on is one lettered HGL – Henry G. Lewis.

courtesy AMEC

Steam Ship Co. Ltd., with offices in London, Newcastle, Swansea, Cardiff, Paris and Genoa, so there would be little difficulty in predicting its end use. Better known is the distribution of the products of the coke works, of which a trainload almost daily went to the British Thompson Houston factory at Rugby. Several photographs exist showing numerous Bedwas Coke wagons in the railway yards at Rugby, including a rare 1939 colour photograph of a rake of these vehicles, painted red, intermingled with those of J. C. Abbott & Co. of Birmingham, whose own wagons emptied to Bedwas and who negotiated the contract. Abbot's were also sales agents for Bedwas and had some of their own wagons lettered for 'Bedwas Coke' or 'Bedwas Coal'.

Coal was first lifted at Bedwas in 1912, and it was in June of that year than an order was placed with the Gloucester company for 360 new 12-ton wagons, paid for in cash. A further order was recorded the following month for a further 360 wagons, it is possible that this may have been a duplicated entry in the company minutes. Of the first 360 wagons, number 47 was registered by the GWR, No. 32318, and was still in pooled service in 1944. The Bedwas Coke plant of British Benzol & Coal Distillation Ltd ordered in 1929 from Gloucester RC&WCo. 200 massive 20-ton capacity coke wagons, taken

out on deferred payment terms at £26 11s. 8d. per annum each, followed by five fourteen-ton tank wagons. In turn, some 12-ton wagons were purchased from Charles Roberts in 1928 and one of these, No. 621, painted light grey with the same lettering layout, is the subject of two available models and is illustrated in Bill Hudson's *Private Owner Wagons*, Volume 1.

For modellers, the above details show that they would be correctly depicted on any model railway representing the route between South Wales and Rugby, the most likely route being via Bristol and Birmingham. Domestic sales were significant for heating boilers etc especially in schools and offices (by contract) and competed with local gas companies anywhere. That a colour picture of Bedwas wagons in red in 1939 exists is a suggestion that those originally painted grey may have ended up in that livery.

The colliery was one of the last surviving deep mines in South Wales and was closed in 1985, after consistently producing in the vicinity of half a million tons of coal a year right up until the 1970s.

MODELS : 12-ton coke wagon (different livery) Mainline, Bachmann, Powsides

No. 1 of the Birchenwood fleet was the first of three built in 1904 in the workshops of Robert Heath & Co. Ltd of Kidsgrove. It has seven planks, side, end and bottom doors, and brakes one side only. The wagon was painted red with white letters shaded black. Italic lettering reads '*Empty to Birchenwood Sidings, Harecastle, N.S.R.*'.

courtesy Mr Allan C. Baker

BIRCHENWOOD COLLIERY Co. Ltd

THE Birchenwood collieries at Kidsgrove, in North Staffordshire, were connected to the North Staffordshire Railway about a half mile east of Kidsgrove Station, the junction being at the northern end of the Harecastle tunnels, which carried the railway and parallel canal from Stoke-on-Trent. The Birchenwood Colliery was connected to the Potteries Loop, which avoided the tunnel and served considerable industry and coal mines.

The Birchenwood Colliery Co. Ltd was formed in 1892 to take over the existing collieries of the Kidsgrove Steel Iron & Coal Company and in 1895 was working the Clough Hall, Harecastle and Speedwell pits. It was at this time a subsidiary of Robert Heath & Co. Ltd, a noted and substantial name in Potteries industry. By 1923 production had reached 325,000 tons of coking, gas, steam, household and manufacturing coal per annum with a personnel of 2,350. The company also owned a coking and by-products plant and a brickworks capable of producing 150,000 bricks per week. In 1931, the collieries, then almost worked out, were closed, although the brickworks and coking plant remained in production operated and managed by a partnership between three prominent Potteries coal companies, Sneyd, Norton & Biddulph and Chatterley Whitfield.

It was the surviving businesses that were responsible for Birchenwood wagons remaining in circulation long after the collieries had closed. The coking plant was still a viable business and amongst all of the collieries which incorporated such a facility, Birchenwood owned an unusually large percentage of coke wagons in its fleet. These, of course, would remain in use with their original livery for long after the colliery was closed, carrying coke and other by-products. There were a number of tank wagons included, some were built early in the twentieth century by Charles Roberts: No's 8, 9 and 10 in 1914 and No.11

two years later. During the first world war they were regularly sent to the Birmingham Gas Works carrying Benzol, sold via Wilson Carter & Pearson Ltd when the contracted supplier, the Grassmoor Colliery, was unable to maintain such supplies. In 1944, wagon No. 221, registered with the North Staffordshire Railway (registered No. 2894) was recorded as repaired and rebuilt.

Taking the known distribution pattern of other collieries in the area, the principal markets for Birchenwood coal would have been the Midlands, Cheshire, Lancashire, Shropshire, north Wales and export trade to Ireland from both Birkenhead and Liverpool. Birchenwood gas coal was supplied to the Coventry Corporation, Borough of Stafford, City of Birmingham Gas Works and to the Middlewich Gas Light & Coke Co; the latter delivered from Harecastle and Birchenwood via the Trent & Mersey Canal.

After the collieries closed the coal wagons may have been drafted to coke and brick traffic, there is already proof that some were running in the Birchenwood livery well into the war years. The above distribution is suggested, but these wagons may at times have travelled to London for the Birchenwood Gas Coal & Coke Co Ltd, as it was latterly.

Between 1892 and 1911, 1,163 wagons were operated by the company. Included were at least 250 coke wagons, although the actual figure cannot be established as not all coke wagons were identified separately. In May 1917 the Company owned 1,096 wagons and was buying 105 on hire-purchase. In May 1918, however, a BoT statement credited them with only 645 wagons, all 10-ton.

MODELS : Powsides

18

CITY OF BIRMINGHAM ELECTRICITY SUPPLY DEPARTMENT

THE rival corporation-owned utility to the City of Birmingham Gas Department, which was extensively described in *Private Owner Wagons: A First Collection*, dated from the 1st January 1900 when the city purchased the Birmingham Electric Supply Co. The company had begun the supply in April 1891 but it was ten years later that the very flimsy surviving records commence and indicate that coal was purchased in that year.

The Department operated initially two power stations, Nechells, alongside the Nechells Gas Works beside the Midland Railway line from Birmingham to Derby, and also served by the Birmingham & Warwick Canal, and Summer Lane, a site beside the Birmingham & Fazeley Canal near where the City Hospital stands today. By 1924 there was also a station at Chester Street. The larger and more modern power station at Hams Hall, between Water Orton and Whitacre Junction on the ex-Midland Railway line from Birmingham to Nuneaton, was opened in 1929. Upon completion of Hams Hall, Summer Lane was gradually phased out.

Up until 1916, all coal was delivered by boats from collieries in Leicestershire, Warwickshire and Cannock Chase to both Nechells and Summer Lane, the latter being served exclusively by canal for its entire operating life. It was in 1916 that a siding was laid into the Nechells Power Station from the Tame and Rea group of sidings at Washwood Heath, and deliveries of coal by rail commenced.

The wagon fleet was launched concurrently with the purchase of fifty 12-ton wagons from the Buxton Lime Firms, built by Gittus of Penistone. There are no surviving details of the origin of the remainder, the few that have been recorded suggest that they were purchased secondhand in the same manner as the original fifty. Regardless, by 1933 there were 314 wagons in service, and the Department also owned seventy canal boats, which were used to transport coal to the Summer Lane Power Station and apparently also for the transport of breeze (coke dust) from the Birmingham Gas Works.

In contrast to the Gas Department, the procurement of coal supplies was done in such a haphazard manner that the Gas Department coal purchasing committee took over this function for some years. However, by 1933 the Electricity Department resumed responsibility. The only record of coal purchased and its source was in 1933 and is taken from a totally unidentified summary, the origin of which was traced from the signature on an accompanying letter, that of Mr E. J. Jennings, who was at the time Secretary and General Manager.

In direct contrast to coal supplied to the gas works, which had to be of a specific quality and was not mined in the immediate vicinity, that used by the power stations was mainly small coal and slack from collieries within Warwickshire, South Derbyshire, Leicestershire and Cannock Chase.

The majority of contracts were placed with local coal factors but the three principal factors in Birmingham, Messrs J. C. Abbott & Co., Messrs Wilson, Carter & Pearson Ltd, and Messrs Evesons (Coals) Ltd, took little or no part in the supply of coal to the Electricity Department, whose preference for smaller operators is obvious.

This photograph of wagon No. 3669 is one of few known photographs of any wagon belonging to this utility. The fleet of a little over 300 wagons was purchased secondhand and the wagon is in such a poor condition that any further identification is impossible. The body colour is unknown but the lettering is white shaded black.

R. J. Essery collection

Contracts for coal for delivery in 1933 totalled some 400,000 tons, and were awarded as follows:

CONTRACTOR	TONS	ORIGIN
City of Birmingham Gas Dept.	52,000	coke dust. (breeze)
Samuel Barlow Coal Co., B'ham	6,250	Ansley Hall (near Nuneaton)
	7,800	Minorca (Measham, Leics)
	6 boats p/w	Holly Bank (Wolverhampton)
	9,500	Pooley Hall (Polesworth, Warks)
	500	Pooley Hall (By boat, Summer Lane)
	15,000	Shipley (Ilkeston, Derbyshire)
Mrs. A. Brockhurst, B'ham	7 boats p/w	Cannock Chase
	5,200	Coleorton (Ashby, Leics)
Alexander Comley Ltd, B'ham	9 boats p/w	Baggeridge (Pensnett, Worcs)
	15,000	Brereton (Cannock Chase)
	28,600	Coventry
	44,200	Halls (Swadlincote, Derbyshire)
	13,000	Kingsbury (Tamworth)
T. & M. Dixon Ltd, B'ham	5,200	Ansley Hall (Nuneaton)
Haunchwood Collieries, Nuneaton	10,400	Tunnel (Nuneaton)
Frank Knight Limited, B'ham	2 boats p/w	Cannock Chase
	6,240	Arley (Nuneaton)
	26,000	Birch Coppice (Tamworth)
Leamore Coal & Coke Co., B'ham	26,000	Baddesley (Atherstone, Warks)
	13,000	West Cannock (Cannock Chase)
Leonard Leigh Limited, B'ham	20,000	Cannock & Leacroft (Cannock Chase)
	13,000	Griff (Nuneaton)
	six boats p/w	Hamstead (Birmingham)
Lunt Bros, Birmingham	5,200	Exhall (Bedworth, Warwicks)
	12,000	Newdigate (Bedworth)
Moira Colliery Co., Ashby	15,000	Donisthorpe, Rawdon (Leics) or Church Gresley (Derbyshire)
Pooley Hall Colliery Co., Polesworth	20,800	Pooley Hall (Polesworth)
Spencer Abbott & Co. Ltd, B'ham	9 boats p/w	Aldridge (Walsall)
	6 boats p/w	Warren Hall (Cannock)
D. M. Stevenson & Co. Ltd, B'ham	13,000	Whitwick (Coalville, Leics)
	6,500	Binley (Coventry)
Wilson Carter & Pearson Ltd, B'ham	6,500	Tamworth

p/w = per week

Most boatloads went to the non-rail connected Summer Lane Power Station although there was a huge Telpher installation at Nechells for unloading canal boats. These figures have been simplified from the actual contracts themselves to give an annual requirement from each supplier.

Additionally, there were numerous informal arrangements for the supply of coal from several other collieries and spot purchases were regularly made at the Birmingham Coal Exchange, the latter a lengthy list which features many collieries not under annual contract, including Butterley, Pleasley, Shirebrook, Mapperley, Conduit, South Leicester, Cannock Old Coppice, Denby, Netherseal, and Sandwell Park.

Of the above contractors, Samuel Barlow Coal Co. Ltd was one of the most famous canal carriers in the country with a substantial fleet of immediately recognisable boats, but also operated a small fleet of railway wagons, several of which were hired from the Gloucester company, often for short periods during the winter when the canals were 'stopped' and all water-borne traffic ceased. Leonard Leigh Ltd were also a noted operator of coal-carrying canal boats.

Alexander Comley Ltd, Halls, Whitwick, Coventry, Griff, South Leicester, Kingsbury and Moira Colliery Companies and Spencer Abbott & Co. Ltd were featured in *Private Owner Wagons: A First Collection*. Haunchwood Collieries Co. is featured in this volume.

The above shows that the LMS had a stranglehold on the company's inward coal traffic,. most of which would have been funnelled through Burton-upon-Trent from the south Derbyshire and Leicestershire collieries, and through Nuneaton for coal obtained from the Warwickshire coalfield for both Hams Hall and Nechells. The strategic position of the Hams Hall Power Station could have been influenced location-wise by the immediate rail access to both railways. Traffic from the Baddesley, Kingsbury and Birch Coppice collieries would join the Derby to Birmingham main line from the mineral branch at Kingsbury. All traffic for Nechells was specifically directed to the Tame and Rea group of sidings at Washwood Heath. Coal from the Cannock area would most likely have been worked via Bescot or via Walsall and Water Orton for those collieries accessible to the Midland Railway Walsall Branch prior to the 1923 grouping.

Of the company's wagons, surviving records of rebuilds in an LNER Register show the following wagons of varying registrations were rebuilt and re-registered:

3192	LNWR 13289
3083	GWR 3621
3296	GWR 50928
3291	GWR 49098
4049	GWR 57951
3598	LNWR 12262
3336	GWR 19380
4251	Moy, Colchester 1924 formerly Bolsover 5740

A colliery gate record of wagons owned by the corporation taken at the Donisthorpe Colliery of the Moira Colliery Company showed that the following wagons were in the colliery yard on December 12th 1938: 3663, 3685, 3117, 3118, 3119, 3103, 3665, 3674, 3563, 3679, 3684, 3115, 3039, 3568, 3041 and 3670.

Assuming the demand for electric power in Birmingham had grown at the same velocity as that at Nottingham it can be safely assumed that the consumption of coal at the Birmingham power stations would have soared to around three-quarters of a million tons by 1939. Luckily slack coal was in plentiful supply at nearby collieries and the fact that the furthest regular supplier was only forty miles distant was a weighty factor in the company's wagons boasting a relatively short average journey time of a little over eight days, in contrast to the deplorable statistic of fourteen days experienced by its neighbouring Gas Department.

MODELS : None

W. H. BOWATER Ltd

THIS company was founded, as far as can be ascertained, in the late 1880s with a head office in Exchange Buildings, Birmingham and within thirty years it had, according to its advertising, expanded into three continents. It was headed by W. H. Bowater of Birmingham, not to be confused with dentist Alderman Sir W. H. Bowater, for many years Lord Mayor of that city.

Whilst on the surface it appeared to be a medium sized coal contractor with a small number of contracts for local gas works and electricity generating stations, a single advertisement in a 1923 trade journal reveals a very substantial business, with branches at London, Liverpool, Hull, Newcastle upon Tyne, Glasgow, Cardiff, Swansea, Leeds, Manchester and Bristol in the British Isles; Rotterdam and Paris in Europe; Durban in South Africa (where the company was the sole selling agents for the Transvaal & Natal Collieries Limited) and New York in the United States.

A transaction of 14,000 tons of coal recorded at the Wath Main Colliery does not show which of Bowater's branches that it was destined for, and neither are there any further details of the company's involvement in supplying the War Office, The Admiralty, Foreign Governments and the principal railways both home and abroad that they boasted of.

On the domestic front and in the Birmingham area, the company had depots at Soho Wharf, Soho Pool, Tysley, Tysley Wharf, Kings Heath, Hagley Street and Bridge Street. To supply the Birmingham area alone, the following collieries were

No. 1145 was a 12-ton eight-plank side, end and bottom door wagon built by G. R. Turner of Langley Mill. No further details of the wagon are available, but the manufacturer built a similar batch of wagons in 1915, No's 1351 to 1400, painted 'Birmingham, Hull, Liverpool'. The livery appears to be a dark red body, black ironwork and plain white letters. *Midrail Photographs*

patronised: Great Wyrley, Cannock, East Cannock, West Cannock, (Cannock Chase); Pinxton, Swanwick (Derbyshire) Ellistown, Desford, Ibstock, (Leics.) Welbeck, (Notts.) Netherseal (South Derbyshire), Kingsbury and Nuneaton (Warks.).

In the early part of the twentieth century Bowaters were substantial customers of the Bullcroft Colliery (see page 28) and also contractors to the Cannock & Hednesford Gas Company, drawing coal from the Clay Cross collieries in Derbyshire and the Fenton Colliery in Staffordshire.

During the coal strikes of 1921 and 1926 the company imported substantial quantities of coal from Germany, which was sold to several gas works and industries, including Leicester and Nottingham. The latter accepted a delivery of 1,500 tons of Saar coal at £4 7s. 0d. per ton at wharf, Immingham, to which wagon hire and rail freight charges had to be added. The going local price in 1921 was £1 10s. 6d. a ton at pit. Surprisingly, there are no extant records of Bowater importing coal from the United States where it had strong advertised connections with the local industry, although several other coal factors did so.

Records of the company's existence ceased in 1929, when it was no longer listed in any directory. That it suddenly disappeared suggests a merger or absorption with another company, one unconfirmed indication is that it was taken over by Stockwood Rees, the Swansea ship-broker.

A hundred 12-ton mineral wagons 3501-3600 were built by Midland RC&W in 1924 and registered by the GWR and a further twenty 12-ton mineral wagons 2550-2569 are said to have been built by Bowaters themselves between May 1925 and March 1926. Registered by the GWR.

MODELS : None

A number of Bowater wagons can be seen in the background on page 110 of *Private Owner Wagons: A First Collection* at Washwood Heath, Birmingham.

A sketch of W. H. Bowater which appeared with the following particulars: '…he inherited the coal business which is one of the best known in the district. It is, however, due to his own untiring efforts that it has assumed its present proportions…'

BRADBURY, SONS & Co. Ltd

THE company was established in 1859, with offices in London, Southampton and Cardiff. The head office for a time was at 7 Victoria Street, London under the name of Bradbury & Co. Several reorganisations took place subsequently, and the name was changed first to Bradbury, Sons and Co. (1920) Limited. The operations of the 1920 company appear to have been very widespread, branches being then located at Glasgow, Newcastle, Hull, Southampton, Swansea, Cardiff, Newport and abroad. The final company title was adopted in 1928. By 1933 they had become an associated company of Gueret, Llewellyn & Merrett Ltd – GLM – although continuing to use their own name until at least 1938.

The Southampton branch of the company is the only one whose trading records can still be found, for the company was for many years a contractor to the Southampton Borough Council for the supply of coal to various departments, in particular the pumping stations of the waterworks, where for twenty years, 1901 to 1920, coal was supplied from the Dowlais and Bwllfa collieries in South Wales. Other Southampton Council departments were supplied with coal from the Abergeli Colliery.

The company appears to have owned a substantial fleet, many of the early wagons were built by Hurst Nelson. At least 1,101 wagons were built for this firm from 1923 to 1928, as follows: 901-1000 Stableford; 1001-1050 Roberts; 1051-1100 Rose Wentworth; 1121-1170 Birmingham (Hired); 1171-1270 Birmingham (Hired); 1271-1370 Stableford; 1371-1570 Stableford; 1571-1670 Birmingham (Hired); 1671-1720 Rose Wentworth; 1721-1920 Birmingham (Hired); 1922-1971 Rose Wentworth; 8050-8100 Roberts.

The records of the Birmingham RC&W Co. state that the wagons marked '(Hired)' above were built for the British Wagon Co. and painted in Bradbury's livery. Most appear to have been registered by the LMS under Bradbury's name, however, suggesting that they were on 'redemption hire' or hire-purchase terms rather than simple hire. (The exception was the first batch, 1121-1170). It is possible that other wagons were being bought on similar terms. The first 280 built in 1923-24 were to the 1907 RCH Specification but the remainder were 1923 Specification. All were registered by the LMS and all were 12-ton all-timber mineral wagons except that the 51 from Roberts in 1927-28 utilised secondhand ex-WD steel underframes.

The Southampton and Portsmouth branches also traded for some distance into the countryside. Orders noted with the Cardiff colliery agent Evans and Reid in 1938 for coal from the Partridge Jones collieries include a 225 ton delivery direct to Romsey, Hants; and a 618 ton order for the Somerset County Council at Yeovil.

Coal mined in South Wales and consumed in Southampton was generally sent by sea, as was coal from the Durham coalfield for the Southampton Gas Works. However, despite Bradbury's connections with the shipping trade and their patronising of Welsh collieries, it appears that some Welsh coal was delivered by rail as both wagons illustrated emptied to Welsh collieries. Indeed, the opening of the Severn Tunnel was hailed in Southampton as a means of better access to South Wales coal. Outside of London, Southampton was the biggest seaport in the country in terms of coal received, the 1912 figures were around three-quarter of a million tons.

MODELS : No. 1493, Powsides

Wagon No. 2018 was built in 1903 by Hurst Nelson Ltd of seven planks with side and end doors, brakes one side, inside diagonal bracing and the typical Hurst Nelson pair of heavy timber door stops, which have drilled recesses to accommodate the heads of the bolts on the door hinge straps. It is loaded with what appears to be magnificent hand selected large lumps of Welsh steam coal. The wagon has a black body with plain white lettering. Italic lettering on the left reads '*In case of breakdown advise 7 Victoria S^t, S.W.*' and at right '*Empty to Dowlais Coll^y Via Rogerstone G.W.R.*'. The three plates on the solebar read, from left, 'For repairs advise Chatsworth Wagon Works, Chesterfield, Hurst Nelson & Co. Ltd'; registration plate LSWR No. 906; and 'Bradbury, Sons & Co. Limited Owners'. The fleet number is repeated on the fixed end. The Dowlais Colliery of Guest, Keen and Nettlefolds Ltd was located at Merthyr Tydfil.

Kidderminster Railway Museum

No. 1493 is also a Hurst Nelson product of 1901, again of seven planks with side and end doors, brakes one side and inside diagonal bracing. In this instance the wagon is finished with a black body, white letters and blue shading. Covering the empty return instructions is a hand written label which cannot be fully deciphered, but the top line reads 'When Empty'. From the left the first two plates on the underframe, read 'For repairs advise Chatsworth Wagon Works, Chesterfield, Hurst Nelson & Co. Ltd'; registration plate LSWR No. 393 of 1901, and the third is the manufacturer's plate.

courtesy HMRS, ABN 305

Briggs' wagon No. 4008 is from a batch of 300 numbered 4001 to 4300 and built by Charles Roberts in 1927. It has eight planks, side, end and bottom doors and was registered with the LMS. The wagon number is also shown on the end door and the italic lettering bottom right reads 'Empty to Whitwood Collieries Sidings L M S & L N E.'. *courtesy HMRS*

HENRY BRIGGS, SONS & Co. Ltd

THE several collieries of Henry Briggs, Sons & Co. Ltd were to be found in an area around Normanton and Methley, Yorkshire, to the south east of Leeds, and served by a concentration of railways of various pre-grouping origins which ensured access to most parts of the country. The company also owned a large chemical and by-products plant at Whitwood. Some of the collieries also had access to the nearby Aire and Calder Navigation, which allowed coal to be tipped into large compartment boats operated in trains hauled by tugs to Goole Docks for transhipment to ocean going colliers. The various collieries were (in 1938):

WATER HAIG	on the former Midland Railway Leeds to Normanton line near Woodlesford.
SAVILE	(also spelt Saville) on the former Midland Railway near Methley.
WHITWOOD	three collieries, Haigh Moor, Silkstone and Beeston on the former North Eastern Railway York to Normanton line near Castleford and the Midland and Lancashire & Yorkshire Methley Branch. (This was also the site of the chemical and by-products works.)
SNYDALE	connected to the LMS.

By this time the collieries combined were producing 1.5 million tons of gas, steam, household and manufacturing coal every year. In 1939 the Peckfield Colliery of the Micklefield Coal & Lime Company was acquired. Exports via Hull in 1912 amounted to 300,000 tons.

The Whitwood Colliery was also noted as a long term home for two ex-Mersey Railway condensing locomotives, *Dorothy* and *Whitwood*, both 2-6-2 tank engines built in 1892 by Kitsons (works numbers 3394 and 3395), purchased in 1904 and still going strong in 1947, although not as famous as the surviving 0-6-4 Beyer Peacock *Cecil Raikes* at Shipley in Derbyshire. Also on the roster were six even older 0-6-0 saddle tanks which started life on the North Eastern Railway, four of which were still at work in 1947 at the ripe old age of 72 years.

Markets for Briggs' coal were principally in Lancashire and Yorkshire, principal customers being large coal factors and the CWS of Manchester, which ordered considerable quantities of household coal for its various branches, Bingley, Keighley and Carnforth each taking several wagons a week. The Eclipse Mill at Rochdale contracted for 10 wagon loads a week, but apart from two small clients in London, little was sent to other parts of the country. One shipment noted was an 80-ton lot to Chandlers Ford in 1936, account Wm. Cory & Sons. For a time the Gas Light & Coke Co. of London contracted for 50,000 tons a year, which was sent by sea via Goole, as was a contract for a similar amount for the South Suburban Gas Co. The company also had a regular contract with the gas works at

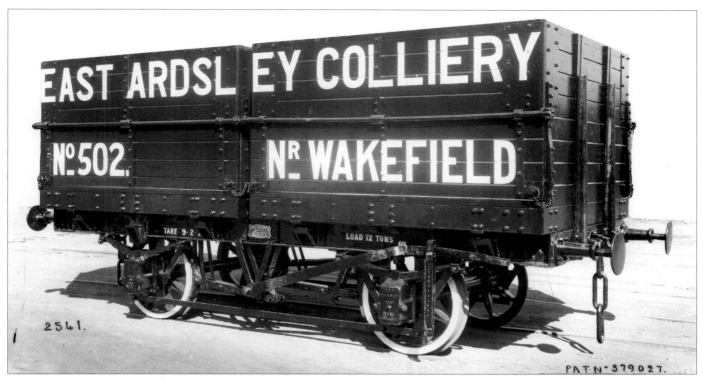

No. 502, although lettered for the East Ardsley Colliery, (note that the letters 'E' and 'Y' are painted on the wagon's corner plates) was actually owned by Briggs and is one of three built experimentally in 1932 by Charles Roberts for traffic to the landsale depot of that colliery from Briggs own collieries. From the photograph it can be seen that it is of a very unusual design with two compartments, each with a horizontally hinged door with pin and chain fastening specifically designed for discharging by means of a side tipping mechanism. Of patent design, it has an extremely sturdy steel body sill, steel end posts and a wooden superstructure of considerably greater strength than one would expect to find in a standard wagon reflected in the unusually high tare weight, which suggests that some very rough handling was expected. Unfortunately there are no further references in the company minutes which would enlighten us further on its construction, or which would tell us that a further series of identical design was built with Briggs in-house lettering (wagon No. 5005, *below*) and most likely used to carry coal to the Aire & Calder Canal where there were side tipping discharge facilities. Small letters to bottom left read 'WHEN EMPTY TO SAVILE COLLIERY VIA METHLEY, LMS.'. It may be that these wagons were specifically designed with two compartments for compatibility with unloading facilities, each compartment being of a similar width to the end door of a standard wagon.

both courtesy HMRS

This Hurst Nelson built wagon, No. 1583, is from one of a series of orders, totalling 450 vehicles, delivered between 1904 and 1908, numbered 1301 to 1750. The seven-plank side and end door wagon appears to be painted light grey with black letters shaded red and with red ironwork. A number of photographs of wagons in such unusual liveries from this builder exist and it is considered that these were for photographic purposes only, or possibly as sample wagons sent to the prospective customer for evaluation. That this was done frequently could even indicate that sales were better when presented as such and then when it came to the nitty-gritty a better price was offered without such a flamboyant appearance, which was eagerly swallowed by prospective purchasers. This may have contributed to the success of Hurst Nelson in supplying wagons all over England. It certainly worked with Briggs as a large order was forthcoming and although there are no records to indicate in which livery they were delivered it is considered, that without evidence to the contrary, the Briggs standard – and very plain – livery was adopted. Intending modellers should take note.   *courtesy HMRS*

Bradford.

Other unusual deliveries were:

11.03.1937	Renwick Wilton & Dobson, wagon No. 66 to Lawrence & Co, Fratton
19.05.1937	Peake, Oliver & Peake wagon No. 543 to Shorncliffe
04.05.1934	Evesons, London direct delivery to Fratton
	CWS London 53 tons, six wagons direct to CWS Cambridge
24.10.1937	John Heaton Manchester wagon No. 1391 to Bury Gas Works

Some records of the company still exist, and there are several references to the wagon fleet, the following of which have been recorded.

21.12.1926	Had on hire from Charles Roberts 100 12-ton wagons No's 1301 to 1400
24.01.1927	Purchased secondhand from Charles Roberts 20 hoppered wagons, ten each for Snydale and Savile
06.03.1928	On hire from Wm Morris, Newport, 119 wagons. Monthly billings based on individual earning of each wagon
11.11.1928	Some wagons belonging to Low Laithes Colliery in traffic on short term hire
20.11.1931	Trials with all steel hoppers to Batley commenced (these appear to be those built for coal merchant Norman Jackson in that town)
25.04.1932	Three special side tipping wagons (No's 500 to 502) built by

	Charles Roberts for landsale traffic on trial, these were lettered for East Ardsley Colliery
04.05.1934	Wagon No. 4913 trialed with creosoted finish

For much of its existence the company patronised Charles Roberts for its new wagons, a major exception being orders placed with Hurst Nelson in 1904 and 1908 for 450 wagons delivered over a period of five years. These were registered with the Midland Railway and numbered between 1301 and 1750 of which No. 1583 can be seen above. New coke wagons were delivered to the Whitwood Works by Roberts, a total of 23 with scattered running numbers in 1914 and registered with the North Eastern Railway, followed by fifteen from Stevens of Doncaster (No's 201 to 215) and 45 from Roberts (No's 231 to 275) in 1931 and registered with the LNER.

In 1924 fifty wagons were ordered from R. Y. Pickering numbered 2601 to 2650 followed by 25 from S. J. Claye numbered 2676 to 2700. Then came a huge order to Charles Roberts totalling 950 wagons numbered 4001 to 4950 and delivered between 1927 and 1929.

Some idea of the amount of coal shipped in February 1937 to various areas can be judged by the tonnage despatched collectively. Old habits die hard, pre-grouping descriptions of the various railways serving the collieries were still being used fourteen years after they had disappeared officially forever:

Midland	36,908
North Midland	7,605
London	7,405
Shipments	15,635
Lancashire & Yorkshire	16,514
North Eastern	5,265
office (this is not defined)	13,654

Judging by contracts registered in that year for specific types of coal for direct delivery to consumers, the principal clients were James Wilby of Pontefract; Sivewright Bacon of Leeds; Smith Parkinson & Cole of Bradford; John Heaton of Manchester; Laneside Coal Co. of Rochdale; Nuttall & Whitehead of Great Harwood and Edwin Scarborough of Halifax. London traffic was only a shadow of its former self, down to only a third of what had been sent to the capital ten years earlier: what was still offering was represented by Hoare, Gothard & Bond, Herbert Howes, and Wm Cory & Sons. These individual records are far from complete and only represent around a quarter of the collieries production. A model of the Whitwood Chemical Works wagon is available, it would probably have been restricted to the industrial areas of Lancashire and Yorkshire.

MODELS : Briggs, none;
Micklefield : Powsides

The wagon lettered for the Micklefield Coal & Lime Co. Ltd was built by Charles Roberts in 1906 as part of an order for 100 wagons numbered 400 to 499. It has six wide planks, side, end and bottom doors and this photograph, taken as it left the works, is in total contrast to one of these wagons in service some thirty years later, described by Bill Hudson in his *Private Owner Wagons*, Vol. 3 (Oxford Publishing Co., 1984) where the company motif has been added to the wagon door and the wagon number transferred to the bottom left corner. The Micklefield company was taken over by Henry Briggs in 1939, which suggests that little re-branding took place. *Wakefield Collection*

Below: The train of Briggs' wagons hauled by the ex-Mersey Railway 2-6-2 tank locomotive *Dorothy* has hanging on the first wagon a placard which cannot be read, but it is understood that it refers to a consignment of coal for a CWS location in either Lancashire or Yorkshire in 1936. The leading wagons are No's 4657 and 4579, followed by 4714, all from an order for 650 wagons delivered by Charles Roberts in 1929 and numbered 4301 to 4950. They were painted with a black body and plain white lettering. *Wakefield Collection*

BULLCROFT MAIN COLLIERIES Ltd

THE Bullcroft Colliery, near Carcroft a short distance north of Doncaster, was opened in 1912 by the Bullcroft Main Collieries Co. Ltd, formed in 1908, who simplified their name in 1913. It worked the Barnsley Bed seam of high quality steam coal, in the early years much of which was sold to The Admiralty for the Royal Navy steam fleet. It was served by the Great Northern and Great Central West Riding and Grimsby joint line giving access to the Humber ports and the industrial areas of Yorkshire and Lancashire, and a direct route to the London markets via the Great Northern main line.

Also under the same directorate was the Markham Main Colliery, also near Doncaster, and for a time the Ramcroft Colliery near Palterton on the Midland Railway near Bolsover in Derbyshire, the latter being short lived as it was closed in 1937. Bullcroft worked until 1970, when it was merged with nearby Brodsworth.

By 1932, with a workforce of 2,600, production reached a million tons a year, and if all of this was transported by rail it would mean 20,000 tons a week, or between 2,000 and 2,500 wagon loads, over 300 wagon loads a day.

In 1936 a rationalisation of colliery ownership in the Doncaster area resulted in two major amalgamations, that which formed Amalgamated Denaby Collieries (see page 47) and that which formed Doncaster Amalgamated Collieries Ltd, consisting of Bullcroft, Brodsworth, Yorkshire Main, Firbeck Main, Hickleton and Markham Main. Of the others, Thorne and Askern remained in their original ownership, as did

Harworth and Bentley of Barber Walker & Co. Doncaster Amalgamated Collieries Limited was represented by the selling agency Doncaster Collieries Association, which co-ordinated the sale of its coal.

With the markets for Bullcroft coal being so widespread, the wagons could have been seen anywhere in the Lancashire and Yorkshire areas, on the Great Northern and Great Eastern lines between Doncaster and London, and at the east coast ports. A 'colliery gate' record of coal sent to docks for export, including that from Bullcroft, taken on July 22nd, 1937, shows the following:

5 wagons to Alexandra Docks, Hull, account Lowe, Stewart and Co.
22 wagons to Hull account W. R. Johnston and Sons
16 wagons to Immingham account W. R. Johnston and Sons
2 wagons to Immingham accout Williams and Co.
9 wagons to Immingham account W. R. Johnston and Sons
9 wagons to Immingham account Evans and Reid
16 wagons to Immingham account Pyman Bell
10 wagons to Immingham account Burns and Lindeman

Records of each individual wagon number which have been preserved shows that by this time Bullcroft wagons had been intermingled with those of the other members of the Doncaster Amalgamated Collieries group, and between the merger would have been pooled with those of the others. Probably very few would have been rebranded before the 1939 compulsory pooling.

The earlier wagons of the company, such as No. 757, were identified with the portrait of a bull on the left-hand side of the door. It is difficult to determine who built the wagon in the first place, the registration plate is indecipherable, but the other plate on the underframe bears the large initials 'SES', indicating S. E. Stevens of Doncaster who may have overhauled it. Tucked in under the left-hand side knee is a Charles Roberts' plate which appears to read Horbury Junction, Wakefield. Most of the italic lettering is too worn to read. The wagon had a red body with white letters shaded black. The bull was white, edged in black and all vertical ironwork was also black. The use of the graphic started with 100 12-tonners from Ince. Next came 'BULLCROFT MAIN' in an arc, rather than the straight 'BULLCROFT' seen opposite. *courtesy HMRS*

Colliery delivery records exist from 1912 to 1919, and show that The Admiralty was the biggest customer, other major accounts being:

Bee, Bingham, Doncaster

Edward Bannister, Grimsby

W. H. Bowater, Birmingham

Bradbury & Sons, London

Wm Cory, London and Hull

Cragg, Ramskir & Catley, Doncaster

Cornwall, London

J. Fielding, New Hay

James Edge, Manchester (the colliery's second biggest customer, around 6,000 tons a month)

W. Fletcher and Co., Leeds and Bradford

Great Grimsby Coal, Salt & Tanning Company

J. Hargreaves, Leeds

Adam Lee, Oldham

Herbert Johnston, Ashton-under-Lyne

Mellonie & Goulder, Ipswich

W. T. Marshall, Hull

Parkgate Iron and Steel, Rotherham

W. J. Russell, Hull

C. K. Smith, Dukinfield

D. M. Stephenson, Hull

J. & J. Taylor, Batley

J. Wilby, Pontefract

William Wood, Huddersfield

Worms and Co., Grimsby

M. Whittaker, Leeds

Exports from Hull alone totalled 300,000 tons in 1913 but the war ended this trade for some years. Coal was also sold to several railway companies: the LNWR, North Eastern, Midland, Great Northern, Great Central, and Great Eastern. It was also sold direct to steamship companies Elders Fyffes and Elder Dempster Lines who owned their own collieries in South Wales (see page 54).

No. 1900 was a twenty-ton all-steel vehicle built by Charles Roberts. It is understood that this was a sample wagon, others of which were sent to other users for trial purposes, in an attempt to emulate the activities of the Great Western in Wales. That few collieries in Yorkshire or nearby ordered fleets makes for a reasonable assumption that the effort was in vain. The wagon has a red body and white letters shaded black. *courtesy R. S. Carpenter*

MODELS : Farish, Powsides; With bull, Bachmann/Allison

The line-up of 25 new wagons for the colliery was photographed outside the Midland Works at Washwood Heath, Birmingham in 1923. These were eight-plank, side, end and bottom door vehicles and numbered from 1953 upwards. Again they were finished with a red body, lettered in plain white and with black ironwork. In unusually large letters at bottom right 'EMPTY TO BULLCROFT MAIN COLLIERY, DONCASTER'. *Birmingham Central Library*

Purchased secondhand from the Gloucester RC&WCo. in 1933, the wagon illustrated probably cost around £75. Unfortunately this was during a short period from which the Gloucester records, admirably almost complete as they are, have not survived so the number of wagons in the transaction is unknown. It had side, end and bottom doors, seven planks and brakes both sides. The wagon was painted black with white letters shaded red. Italic lettering at bottom left reads 'Loaded to Oswald St., Gas Works Sidings, Burnley.'.

GRC&WCo.

BURNLEY CORPORATION GAS DEPARTMENT

BEFORE nationalisation in 1949, roughly half the British gas industry was in municipal ownership although very few towns were first gas lit by municipal enterprise, Manchester being the notable exception. It was a Company of Shareholders who got things going at Burnley in 1823 and not until 1854 did the Local Authority buy-out a profitable business.

Gas antedates the railway age and Burnley's first gas works at Parker Lane was on the Leeds & Liverpool Canal. Coal arrived in 'Boat Boxes' – lift-off containers which were later seen on railway wagons. Growing demand made the Parker Lane site congested so the latest vertical retorts were erected in 1909 but they were not a success. Being supplied only by canal also limited the choice of coals. Once stability returned after the 1914-18 war, a spacious new site was developed at Oswald Street, between Burnley Central and Brierfield on the Burnley to Skipton line, where the Corporation had private sidings. The new works also reverted to horizontal retorts. All coal now came by rail and more diverse sources were tapped. Coal was purchased mainly from Lancashire and South Yorkshire collieries, and in most instances contractors were entrusted with its procurement from an agreed list.

In the 1920s the works used 60,000 tons of coal a year, of which between 35 and 40,000 were supplied by local collier John Hargreaves. The remaining contracts are somewhat vague, but confirm that 2,000 tons of coal a year from Mitchells Main Colliery in Yorkshire was supplied by James Beswick of Manchester; 2,000 tons of Emley Moor gas coal by J. Mitchell of Todmorden; 2,000 tons of Whitwood by John Heaton of Manchester and 11,750 tons from an unknown source by H. Crossdale, Blackburn.

From the late 1920s the output of Oswald Street Gas Works was supplemented by a supply of coke oven gas from Altham. Unlike Accrington, who shared this bounty, Burnley did continue production albeit at a reduced level. 1938 was typical, with 481 million cubic feet of coal gas made and 543 millions bought in and purified. Coal purchases totalled only 32,475 tons in consequence.

The peak of gas coal production was in the late 1950s, when almost 25 million tons were mined. In 1969, the gas supply of the town of Burton-upon-Trent was transferred from coal gas to natural gas which was piped direct to the town's gas works. This change began to spell the end for the traditional gas works with its retort houses and gasholders.

Apart from the wagons purchased secondhand from Gloucester, nothing else is known of the wagon fleet. Unusually, there was a Sulzer coke-cooling plant at Oswald Street from which surplus steam fed a fireless locomotive which was used for shunting wagons in the sidings.

MODELS : None

BUTE MERTHYR COLLIERIES Co.

THE 1st Marquis of Bute (1744-1814), with the family seat of Mount Stuart on the island of Bute, acquired extensive estates throughout South Wales on his marriage to Charlotte Windsor who was descended from the Earl of Pembroke. They moved to Cardiff in 1766. The 2nd Marquis (1793-1848) began the development of the collieries and also built the first dock at Cardiff in 1838 which became known as Bute West Dock. He therefore laid the foundations of one of the biggest coal shipping ports. On his death in 1848 the title and estates passed to his baby son John who had been born the year before. With the 3rd Marquis being so young the estates were run by trustees. The 3rd Marquis became Rector of St Andrews University and died in 1900. It would seem that it was the 4th Marquis who began to dismantle the Welsh industrial interests.

The collieries of the Marquis of Bute at Treherbert, near the head of the Rhondda Valley, date back to the 1850s and were in operation when the Taff Vale Railway was opened in 1856. When the Rhondda & Swansea Bay Railway arrived in 1894, this was an alternative and very convenient way of shipping coal to additional Bristol Channel ports. The original Bute Colliery was the first to raise steam coal in the Rhondda Valley. In addition to the collieries, the Marquis was also chairman of the Cardiff Railway Company.

By this time the working collieries were Bute Merthyr, or Lady Margaret, at Treherbert, opened in 1877 near the junction of the two railway companies, and Bute itself, a smaller and older colliery a short distance away. A third colliery was Tower between Hirwaun and Aberdare on the Hirwaun Common Railway, a private line which diverged from the Great Western's Vale of Neath line at Hirwaun Pond. The Tower was sold in 1919 to David R. Llewellyn who is referred to several times later in this volume. Tower became part of Welsh Associated Collieries, incorporated in 1930 and then became part of Powell Duffryn Steam Coal Co. Ltd in 1935. The Tower Colliery was closed in 1994 but in the following year was re-opened by a private company with an output of 450,000 tons a year. It is still working and is the last deep mine in Wales. Another Bute colliery was the Tylacoch, alongside the Treorchy Station on the Taff Vale Railway. This was short lived and was closed by 1895. It was revived by United National Collieries in 1917, and closed by 1933. There were several small drift mines around Hirwaun Common under the Bute banner which became part of the Duffryn Aberdare Coal Co. Ltd, which in itself also eventually became part of Powell Duffryn.

The sequence of photographs reproduced here shows the progress not only in wagon design but also in the frequent changes of livery so often encountered with Welsh owners. It also shows that wagons were not always numbered in order of acquisition, a trait that often defies the positive identification of wagons when the builder's and registration plates cannot be interpreted. Fortunately these are all Gloucester built wagons and accordingly the salient details are provided within the photographs. The oldest wagon is No. 299, built in 1881 before the days of wagon registration although it carries a GWR registration plate in the C series and a rectangular Gloucester builder's & owner's plate (Glos. No. 16404). It was actually provided to the order of the Bute Merthyr Smokeless Steam Coal Co. placed in February 1881. It has six planks, side and end doors, chain couplings and dumb buffers at one end. The solitary handbrake was operated by an enormous lever set in a ratchet frame on the wagon body rather than the underframe. The internal dimensions of the body are 14ft 6in. x 6ft 9in. x 3ft 5in. The wagon was painted black with white unshaded letters. The large letters B and M in each bottom corner were red. Italic lettering bottom left reads: 'Empty to Bute Merthyr Collieries Treherbert'. GRC&WCo.

No. 325 was photographed in December 1891, and appears to be from an order for fifty wagons placed in that month. It is a 10-ton, six-plank wagon with an end door only. (The neighbouring Fernhill collieries also operated such wagons.) It has internal dimensions of 14ft 5in. x 7ft 0in. x 3ft 8in. Painted black with white letters, trade marks red letters on white diamond. Small italic lettering to bottom left reads *'Empty to Bute Merthyr Collieries, Treherbert'*.   *GRC&WCo.*

Two other collieries connected with the Bute name were Aberdare Merthyr, also on the Hirwaun Common Railway, and Blaenant, a small and short lived colliery (*circa* 1900 to 1929) near Abernant on the Merthyr Branch of the Vale of Neath line. The Aberdare Merthyr pit was formerly owned by the Hirwaun and Aberdare Steam Coal Co. and sunk in 1860, going bankrupt in 1867. It was taken over by the Aberdare Merthyr Steam Coal Co. and by 1900 had become part of the Bute empire. The Aberdare Merthyr Colliery was sold in 1915 to the Powell Duffryn group and closed in 1916. Between 1898 and 1910, the 4th Marquis relinquished many of his mineral leases to the Rhymney Iron Co., Insoles, Powell Duffryn and Guest, Keen & Nettlefolds as a prelude to the mining empire being dissolved.

By 1920 the Bute collieries in the Rhondda had been absorbed by the United National Collieries Limited.

The Bute's were regular clients of the Gloucester RC&WCo. and from 1882 purchased 810 new wagons as detailed below. No quantity was recorded for his first purchase in 1881.

15.02.1881	Purchased new wagons on 7 years deferred purchase, number not specified
08.08.1882	Secondhand wagons hired weekly, 30 10-ton
10.07.1883	New, purchased over 7 years, 20 10-ton
08.01.1884	New, purchased over 7 years, 50 10-ton
10.02.1891	New over 7 years, 60 10-ton, co. repair
08.12.1891	New over 7 years, 50 10-ton, co. repair
10.07.1895	New over 7 years, 100 10-ton, co. repair
02.02.1895	100 new 10-ton
09.05.1907	New over 10 years, 100 12-ton co. repair
11.11.1911	300 new 10-ton wagons

In addition, long term repair contracts were held for 353 wagons ranging from six-tons to eight tons, dating back to 1881:

13.09.1881	50 8-ton, 7 years
14.06.1887	50 8-ton, 7 years, renewal
12.07.1892	52 8-ton, 20 10-ton, 7 years
10.07.1895	110 10-ton, 7 years, renewal
09.12.1896	1 8-ton, 5 10-ton, 7 years
09.02.1898	50 10-ton, renewal, 7 years
09.11.1898	50 10-ton, 7 years
10.05.1899	20 10-ton, 7 years, renewal
13.01.1904	1 8-ton, 5 10-ton, temporary
09.01.1907	1 8-ton, 55 10-ton, 60 10-ton, 20 10-ton, 7 years renewals
11.02.1918	100 12-ton, 7 years

For modellers, a kit has been issued of a Bute wagon, and for authenticity, should not be used on a layout dating after the mid 1920s. All of the company's wagons would have been repainted in the United National colours, and some would have survived long enough to have been identified as Ocean wagons following the 1935 merger with the Ocean Coal Company.

As well as wagons for their collieries the Butes also had wagons from Gloucester for their other interests including the Bute Docks Company and the Bute Hematite Iron Ore Co.

MODELS : Osborne Models

Wagons numbers 115 and 129 represent a further transition and simplification of the corporate livery being painted black with plain white lettering which clearly states the ownership. There are however, differences between them, the word **BUTE** being spread across the wagon side on No. 115 and compressed on 129. Both were delivered within a few weeks of each other, 115 being photographed in June and 129 in July 1907 and appear to be from the same order as No. 166 (*below*), giving three different liveries from a single order for 100 wagons. Both are 12-ton seven-plank wagons with side and end doors and brakes on one side only, registered with the Great Western Railway and measuring internally 15ft 6in. x 7ft 4in. x 4ft 0in. The italic letters at the bottom left on the two wagons read: '*Empty to Bute Collieries, Cwmbach Sidings, Aberdare.*'. Note the untidy letter '**U**' on No. 115 and also that the wagons have been built with the end door to the right when viewed from the side on which the brake is fitted. This is unusual for Gloucester-built wagons but until this date all those for the Marquis had this feature.

GRC&WCo.

The third wagon, No. 166, was photographed in July 1907 although the only order for 100 wagons was only confirmed in the minutes in August. The empty return instructions show the development of the company away from its original Treherbert base It was a seven-plank wagon of 12-tons capacity with side and end doors and measuring 15ft 6in. x 7ft 4in. x 4ft 0in. Painted black with white letters shaded red. The italic lettering in bottom left-hand corner reads '*Empty to Bute Collieries, Cwmbach Sidings, Aberdare.*'.   *GRC&WCo.*

Photographed in November and December 1911 respectively, No's 700 and 802 are part of an order for 300 wagons and are clearly of 12-ton capacity although the order was written down as being for 10-tonners. Once again there has been a change in the lettering layout although it does appear more consistent through the order. Note the extended base to the letter 'E'. Italics read: '*Empty to Bute Collieries, Aberdare or Rhondda Valley.*' which surely gave those despatching the empties a bit of a quandry! Note the wagons had also reverted to Gloucester's normal practice of end door to the left of braked side. Close study also shows a substantial wooden door stop fitted to the far side.

GRC&WCo.

Both wagons show a lightweight style of lettering which is unlikely to have been applied by a professional painter at a wagon works and appears to be the work of the colliery workshops. No. 1380 has a heavy timber door stop, otherwise its origin is unknown. It is seen being shunted at one of the company's collieries by their locomotive No. 6. Note the shunter on the far left wielding one of the most important tools of the Private Owner area, indeed the entire freight handling system of the railway network in Britain, the shunter's pole.

Kidderminster Railway Museum,
J. H. L. Adams collection

No. 1946 has no identifiable origin, the photograph is believed to have been taken at Epsom in the 1930s. The wagons were painted black with unshaded white letters. Italic letters at the bottom right read: *'Cannock Chase Colliery, Near Walsall'.*
Kidderminster Railway Museum,
J. H. L. Adams collection

CANNOCK CHASE COLLIERY Co. Ltd

THE company was founded in 1859, when its initial owners, Messrs McClean and Chawner, leased a large tract of land in Cannock Chase, to the north of Walsall, Staffordshire, from the Marquis of Anglesea. It operated several collieries in the area which were connected to the various Midland Railway and LNWR mineral branches in the immediate vicinity, and also a private line ran to a wharf on the Wyrley & Essington Canal, which in the days before the railway gave immediate access to Walsall and the industry of Birmingham and environs.

In 1923 four pits were working, No's 2 and 3 at Chasetown; No. 8 to the east of Heath Hayes and No. 9 at Hednesford. The two former were served by the LNWR's Walsall to Wichnor Junction line, which was reached via a private railway to Anglesey Sidings Junction, between Brownhills and Hammerwich stations. The others were connected to the South Staffordshire Branch of the same railway. No. 2 was closed in 1925, the other three continued for many years until nationalisation, producing between them 600,000 tons of coal which was distributed throughout the industrial areas of the West Midlands, and as far afield as Southampton, from where wagons belonging to Peter Stewart were regular visitors according to a

former colliery employee. Cannock coal was also delivered regularly to Shropshire, Herefordshire, Worcestershire, the home counties and the outskirts of London. Coal merchants from the Oxford and Reading areas also patronised Cannock Chase collieries.

Depots were established in Birmingham at Perry Barr and Monument Lane, and at Erdington and Sutton Coldfield. In London the company had sales outlets at the LNWR depot at York Road, Wharf Road, Shepherds Bush, Chalk Farm and West End Lane. The company moved its head office from Brownhills to London in 1933.

In 1867 200 10-ton wagons were obtained from the the Gloucester Wagon Co. In 1878, a supply of ironwork was ordered from Gloucester, so much that it might have been intended for home made wagons. The Colliery did indeed build twelve 13-ton wagons in 1939. They were numbered 1260, 1338, 1744, 1747, 1040, 1113, 1192, 1212, 935, 950, 1110 and 1132. They were registered by the LMS.

MODELS : None

CANNOCK OLD COPPICE COLLIERY

THE village of Cheslyn Hay on Cannock Chase may well be remembered by many generations as the village of the various Hawkins families, who ran just about every trading operation in the entire village, including the colliery and even supplied the church organist. No attempt has been made to establish any blood relationship between the various Hawkins, but a 1932 directory lists the following: Hawkins, A. S., pig breeder; A., grocer; A., china and glass dealer; A. (Mrs), newsagent; C., motor garage; F. W., greengrocer; L. C. H., director of music and church organist; S., grocer and W., general merchant. In later years W. Hawkins became a coal factor and brick and tile merchant. Crowning the whole Hawkins dynasty was T. A. Hawkins, owner of the Cannock Old Coppice Colliery.

The latter was situated between the village of Cheslyn Hay and Watling Street, which in the 1930s was the better known name for what we now know as the A5. The colliery was situated about a mile east of the former LNWR line from Walsall to Rugeley, the junction of the colliery tramway being a short distance to the north of Wyrley and Cheslyn Hay Station. Also served was the Rosemary Tile Works; and both industries had access to a canal basin off the Netherton Branch of the Staffordshire & Worcestershire Canal.

The colliery produced household, manufacturing and steam coal which was distributed mainly in the industrial midlands, but like most Cannock Chase collieries also saw a market in Worcestershire, Herefordshire and as far south as Southampton.

Earlier wagons owned by Hawkins were painted with the owner's name on the top two planks and the colliery name on the fourth plank down, the livery as seen here was probably being used for the first time. Virtually concurrent with the fifteen wagons supplied by the Gloucester company were 25 from Birmingham Railway Carriage & Wagon Co. These were numbered 651 to 675 and registered with the LMS (registration numbers 96318 to 96342). Fifty 12-ton seven-plank wagons with side and end doors only were acquired from the Butterley Company in March and April 1936 and numbered 223-272. Once again registration was by the LMS.

MODELS : None

No. 1022 was built by the Gloucester RC&WCo. as one of an order for 200 wagons placed by H. G. Lewis of Cardiff. Fifteen were sold to Cannock Old Coppice Colliery and numbered from 1016 to 1030 prior to registration with the LMS (No's 95339 to 95353). The wagons had side, end and bottom doors and brakes on both sides. Internally the wagon measures 16ft 1in. x 7ft 7in. x 4ft 4in. It was painted 'Slate colour' with all ironwork bar the diagonal strapping black and with white letters shaded black. The most unusual thing about the livery is that the shading of the lettering is to the left. Italic letters at bottom right read 'Telephone 16 Cannock. Empty to Colliery Sidings, Cannock Branch, L.M.S.Rly.'. The oblong plate on the solebar is a Hall, Lewis repairers plate. *GRC&WCo.*

The coking plant at Llanbradach Colliery during the 1920s. *Pope/Parkhouse Archive*

CARDIFF STEAM COAL COLLIERIES Co. Ltd

THE Llanbradach Colliery of the above company was located on the Rhymney Railway main line between Caerphilly and Ystrad Mynach. In 1911 the company changed its corporate title to Cardiff Collieries Limited. The colliery was a large and long lasting one, regularly producing between 650,000 and 700,000 tons of steam and gas coal each year with a workforce of over 2,200. In addition the company owned a quarry at Pwllpant and an installation of fifty Otto Waste Heat type coke ovens with an output of 100,000 tons in 1938.

Markets were divided almost equally between export and United Kingdom, the bulk of the latter being sold to Welsh industry. Single wagon loads were sent regularly to several industries in the Birmingham area, and to Milford Haven, Builth Wells, Falmouth, Brentford, Bristol, Whitchurch and Brecon. Unlike most Welsh companies, the colliery did not deal through an exclusive agency for its exports, but shipped through several coal exporters, mainly at Cardiff but also at other South Wales ports. Principal exporters were Braithwaite Heslop, Evans & Reid, Corys Trading and Gueret, Llewellyn & Merrett.

By-products were sold mainly in bulk to such clients as Arrow Fuels Ltd, who manufactured a patent fuel and purchased pitch; Tar Residuals Ltd who purchased creosote 10,000 gallons at a time; Bird & Sons of Grangetown, creosote; British Sulphate of Ammonia Residuals, sulphate of ammonia; Chance & Hunt, naptha; and National Benzole, benzol. The tar distillery at the by-product plant closed in the late 1930s. All of the company's shipments to local docks are recorded as being in colliery owned wagons.

The company also produced a small amount of gas coal, the gas works at Cardiff being a regular customer. One sale recorded in 1929 was 1,639 tons to Wilson, Carter & Pearson Ltd of Birmingham which would have most likely been gas coal.

The company's railway wagon fleet was initially obtained from Hurst Nelson in Motherwell as well as from the Gloucester company. It was from the latter in 1894 that the first sale of

new wagons was recorded. Most wagons appear to have been registered with the Rhymney Railway or the GWR, (No. 1028 was registered with the Rhymney, No. 1250) records of which are no longer extant. On many occasions large numbers of wagons were hired, often for short periods, which usually indicates that there were substantial fluctuations in the market and often up to four hundred wagons were required immediately. The following listing of transactions with the Gloucester company will give an indication of how much wagon business was done with one company between 1894 and 1908.

10.04.1894	300 10-ton new, deferred payment seven years
08.08.1894	50 secondhand wagons hired
13.11.1894	130 10-ton wagons hired on weekly basis
13.02.1895	46 10-ton wagons hired on weekly basis
08.01.1895	50 10-ton wagons hired on weekly basis
08.05.1895	70 10-ton wagons hired on weekly basis
11.09.1895	50 10-ton wagons hired on weekly basis
13.12.1895	150 10-ton wagons hired on weekly basis
14.10.1896	50 10-ton wagons hired six months
01.05.1898	100 10-ton wagons hired one month
12.10.1898	113 10-ton wagons hired one month
09.01.1901	200 10-ton wagons hired 33 months
06.09.1901	439 10-ton wagons hired three years
12.01.1904	50 8-ton wagons hired one month
13.07.1904	400 10-ton wagons hired three years
09.10.1907	400 wagons hired six months
11.03.1908	400 10-ton wagons hired one year

A transfer of a Llanbradach wagon exists and their range for such a large colliery could have been considerable, one was photographed at Cromford in Derbyshire in the 1930s.

MODELS : Dragon Models, Osborne Models

The oldest of the two wagons is No. 252, built by Gloucester in 1894, from an order for 300 wagons recorded in April of that year which were the foundation of the companys fleet. It has side and end doors, brakes on one side and seven planks. Internally it measured 14ft 6in. x 7ft 0in. x 4ft 0in. the wagon was painted black with white letters. In italics at bottom left is 'Empty to Llanbradach Colliery, Rhymney Ry.'.

GRC&WCo.

The second wagon, No. 1101, is of more recent vintage and dates back to the earliest part of the twentieth century, probably around 1910 and was built by Hurst Nelson. It is possible that, like others from this maker, it was specifically painted as a sample wagon for approval before an order was placed. It has seven planks, side and end doors, brakes both sides and is of 12-tons capacity. The livery appears to be a medium to dark grey body with unshaded white letters and black ironwork and with the tare weight and capacity painted in the bottom right-hand corner.

courtesy HMRS

CHEMICAL & METALLURGICAL CORPORATION Ltd

Illustrated are three types of tank wagon built by the Gloucester RC&WCo. for specialised transport of chemicals in bulk. No. 133 was photographed in April 1929 and is from an order for thirty such vehicles placed in May the previous year. Its dimensions are: tank, inside diameter 21ft 5in. x 6ft 4in.; overall length 21ft 6in. over headstocks, 24ft 6in. over buffers; width over headstocks 6ft 10in., over crossbraces 7ft 10in.; wheelbase 12ft 0in. The tare weight was 11 tons 12 cwt. Unfortunately Gloucester do not specify what colours the tank wagons they built were painted. Small lettering reads 'RETURN WHEN EMPTY TO ASTMOOR WORKS SIDINGS, VIA WARRINGTON AND ACTON GRANGE, (MANCHESTER SHIP CANAL RLY)'. The rectangular plate on the underframe reads: 'THE CHEMICAL & METALLURGICAL CORPORATION LD, HEAD OFFICE, 701 SALISBURY HOUSE, LONDON EC2.' with the secretary's name in the bottom left-hand corner. The plate to the right of the builders plate is an owner's plate for Wagon Finance in Sheffield.

GRC&WCo.

THE heavy concentration of the chemical and allied industries on the border of Cheshire and Lancashire dates back to the early part of the nineteenth century. Transportation of coal via the Bridgewater Canal and other early Navigations preceded the railway era by several decades, but it was the coming of the railway and later the Manchester Ship Canal which encouraged the pioneers of the alkali industry to set up their factories where not only coal, but limestone and salt were readily available in reasonable proximity so that products used by glassworks, soap factories and dyestuffs factories could be manufactured, and as a bonus these industries were naturally attracted as satellite establishments.

It was in 1862 that Charles Wigg and partners, later to become Wigg Brothers & Steel and even later Wigg & Kenet, commenced producing alkalis in a factory beside the River Mersey and later also served by the Manchester Ship Canal, where wharves were provided. Wigg was also involved in the promotion of the Runcorn Soap & Alkali Company, controlled by the Johnson Brothers, prominent names in local industry, who also owned a coal mine at St. Helens and whose business empire collapsed in a somewhat spectacular manner on both sides of the Atlantic Ocean.

In 1890 an initial amalgamation of 48 of the alkali works in the Widnes/Runcorn area formed United Alkali Co. Ltd and in 1926 the formation of Imperial Chemical Industries Ltd was achieved by the amalgamation of this company with Brunner Mond Ltd, British Dyestuffs Corporation Ltd, and Nobel Industries Ltd. Four years later further amalgamations took place, the former Wigg factory (always known as Wiggs Works in Runcorn) and its subsidiary English Gelatine and Phosphates Limited was placed under the management of United Alkalis, having by this time acquired the trading name of Chemical & Metallurgical Corporation Ltd, which probably dates back to at

The smallest of the tank wagons, No. 36, was designed specifically for the carriage of sulphuric acid. It was of fourteen-ton capacity, registered with the LMS (registration No. 106392) and has the dimensions of: tank inside: 15ft 6in. long by 5ft 8in. diameter; length over headstocks 16ft 6in.; length over buffers 19ft 6in.; width over headstocks 7ft 8in.; width over crossbraces 6ft 3in.; wheelbase 9ft 0in. Tare weight 9tons 5cwt. Once again Gloucester have kept the body colour a secret. Italic lettering at bottom left (the empty return instructions) and that on the rectangular plate on the underframe are the same as No. 133, with the exception of the wagon number. It is somewhat surprising that wagons of this nature and carrying so many dangerous substances were not fitted with continuous brakes: the lack of a large white star on the body indicates that they were not authorised to be hauled in fast goods trains. *Below right* is a detail of the tank end and end stanchions.   GRC&WCo.

least 1924 as this was when railway wagons were first ordered under this name.

The factory produced alkalis, for which the basic raw materials are salt, limestone and coal. Every week the local factories used 2,600 tons of salt alone, to produce 1,800 tons of soda and 665 tons of other by-products. The entire Widnes area used over a million tons of coal a year early in the twentieth century and a heavy pall of smoke hung over the town for much of the time.

The basic finished products consisted of soda ash, chlorine, bleach, ammonia, and chloride of lime, which as bleaching powder was used as a disinfectant and also for the purification of water. Considerable use of these materials was also made by the textile industry, which was heavily concentrated to the immediate north and north-east, its smoking chimneys dominating the skyline of Manchester, Oldham, Rochdale, Bury, Bolton and dozens of other towns large and small.

The Wigg's second factory, latterly called the Astmoor Works, was situated between the swing bridge and the Point Turn Ferry Bridge on the outskirts of Runcorn. The new premises were built between the wars and probably played a crucial role during the second world war. Now demolished, the site has been redeveloped as a leisure area. The works were served by the

Manchester Ship Canal Railway, via the former LNWR sidings at Warrington Acton Grange – to which the Great Western also had access via the joint line with the LMS from Chester to the outskirts of Warrington – and by the Manchester Ship Canal.

In 1928 Wigg's company, Chemical & Metallurgical Industries, placed an order with Charles Roberts of Wakefield for two 14-ton tank wagons. Apart from this order, all of the known wagon fleet was either purchased or hired from the Gloucester RC&WCo., commencing in January 1924 with an order for five 14-ton tank wagons. No further orders were placed until May 1928, when thirty 20-ton tank wagons were ordered, followed by five more in September of the same year.

In the following December a further 35 20-ton tank wagons were ordered, and at the same time a five year hire of twenty 12-ton open mineral wagons was arranged. These were formerly owned by the Neath Abbey Patent Fuel Co. but repossessed by the Gloucester company (see page 88). More wagons were ordered from Gloucester in 1929, two lots of five 14-ton tank

wagons for sulphuric acid traffic in January (No's 20 to 38 even numbers only: registered LMS 106361 to 106365 and 106389 to 106393), and three 18-ton tank wagons in September.

All of these vehicles were painted in the Chemical & Metallurgical livery and upon completion of the takeover by ICI would have been integrated into the varied fleet that was assembled from its constituent companies and eventually assumed a standard livery. The mineral wagons were probably used to carry coal from the pits in the Wrexham-Ruabon or North Staffordshire areas, and possibly from the Lancashire coalfield. The tank wagons, being designed and constructed for carrying dangerous and corrosive materials, would have been used to transport bulk liquid supplies to large users, most likely with their own sidings and integrated unloading facilities. Nothing is known of the areas to which they travelled, but with the intense concentration of industry in the Lancashire and Cheshire area, it is suggested that they were seen mainly in those two counties and possibly also in the industrial midlands.

No. 502, photographed in January 1930 was one of three 18-ton capacity tanks on 20-ton underframes ordered in the previous September. It was designed for the transportation of hydrochloric acid – a solution of the gas of hydrogen chloride in water – a powerful acid used in industry. The 3,374 gallon capacity tank, which was 13ft 6in. in length and 6ft 1in. in diameter, was rubber lined. Other dimensions were length 21ft 6in. over headstocks and 24ft 6in. over buffers; width 6ft 10in. over headstocks and 8ft 3in. over crossbraces. The wheelbase was 12ft. Note the construction of the tank body in three sections with flanged joints – this was due to the difficulties in rubber coating the steel – and the shaped rubber plates over the top of the tank barrel to guard against spillage.
GRC&WCo.

MODELS : Powsides

40

CHESTER UNITED GAS COMPANY

CHESTER was first lit with gas in 1818 but a rival company later built its works on the Roodee. The competitors merged to form the 'United' company in 1858 and chose to develop the Roodee site beside the River Dee. It had no rail access, since the GW and L&NW joint line which crossed the site was on a viaduct. Coal was usually hauled from the Cheshire Line Committee yard at Northgate. The company ran a small fleet of railway wagons, those illustrated are the only ones known as very few records of the company remain.

Sample records of coal contracts show that most came from collieries in North Wales, with a solitary supplier in North Staffordshire and a single source in Yorkshire. The 1938 contracts are detailed below:

Contractor	Quantity	Source
Broughton and Plas Power Collieries Limited	2,000 tons	Bersham
United Westminster Collieries	2,000 tons	
Llay Main Colliery	4,000 tons	
Ruabon Colliery, Ruabon	5,000 tons	
Modern Transport Ltd, Liverpool	9,000 tons	Elsecar
	4,000 tons	Llay Hall
Madeley Collieries Ltd, Leycett	5,000 tons	

Elsecar Colliery, near Wombwell in Yorkshire, was on an LNER mineral branch and the route across the Pennines would have been via the Woodhead Tunnel, and then probably via the CLC lines to Chester Northgate. Madeley was situated at Leycett in North Staffordshire and served by an ex-LNWR branch off the west coast main line south of Crewe, therefore this coal would have been transported via Crewe and Chester. The remaining collieries were in North Wales and being served by the Great Western would have been hauled to Chester by that railway. Therefore these wagons would have been seen in a relatively restricted area, except for an odd trip to Elsecar.

MODELS : None

An order for six wagons was placed with the Gloucester RC&WCo. (No's 24 to 29 as seen above) in 1912. They had seven planks, side and end doors and brakes both sides. Internal dimensions were 15ft 6in. x 7ft 4in. x 4ft 2in. Painted 'lead colour' with white letters shaded black and black ironwork bar the diagonal bracing.

GRC&WCo.

On the 25th January 1923 Charles Roberts received an order for fifty wagons, numbered 700 to 749, with side, end and bottom doors. The livery was somewhat extravagant by Yorkshire standards, and the prominence given to the word 'colliery' in its abbreviated form should be noted. The wagon had internal dimensions of 16ft 0in. x 7ft 5in. x 4ft 3in., and was sheeted using five 7-inch, one 8-inch and one 9-inch planks. It was painted red with black ironwork and white lettering. Italic letters to the right read *'Empty to Shaw Cross Colliery, Ossett Branch, G.N.R.'.*
Wakefield Collection

CRAWSHAW & WARBURTON Ltd

THIS company, based near Dewsbury in Yorkshire, dates back to at least 1861 when it worked the Ridings and Soothill collieries. Twenty years later, its empire also embraced the Shaw Cross, Chidswell and Bates collieries in the immediate vicinity. Between 1897 and 1901 it became a limited company with a registered office at Ridings Road, Dewsbury. The Soothill Colliery should not be confused with nearby Soothill Wood, which was under a different ownership. By 1895, the Bates Pit had been closed and a further colliery named Saville had been opened, and again this should not be confused with the Savile Colliery of Henry Briggs Limited.

In 1913 the only collieries still listed were Shaw Cross, Soothill and Chidswell, all served by the Ossett Branch of the Great Northern Railway, Wakefield to Dewsbury and although the postal address was Dewsbury, the collieries were located closer to Batley itself. The Soothill Colliery was abandoned in 1931 and the Saville Colliery apparently revived, as it reappears in 1938, when the three collieries, Shaw Cross, Saville and Chidswell worked with a total workforce of 720. All were still winding coal at Vesting Day, January 1st 1947.

Like many of the medium sized collieries in the Wakefield–Leeds area, the Crawshaw & Warburton collieries produced gas, household and manufacturing coal. No records of its distribution have survived but based on the known markets of other collieries in the area, most would have been distributed in the industrial areas of Yorkshire with some to Lancashire.

A comparatively remote market for its gas coal was the gas works at Northampton, from whom a contract was won in 1929 for the supply of 4,000 tons. Other gas works customers were those at Bradford, Leeds, Otley, Manchester, Harrogate and Bridlington – the latter specified that its coal was to be delivered only in North Eastern Railway style hopper wagons. Only a relatively small amount of coal, 24,000 tons in 1913, was

exported from Hull, despite the company advertising in Hull trade journals.

MODELS : None

Wagon No. 100 is of a style developed by Charles Roberts and sold to several colliery companies in Yorkshire. It has eight planks and side and end doors. These wagons date from the late 1930s but no record of the actual order could be found so it may be on hire. The wagon was finished with an unpainted treated timber body and black ironwork. The small plate under the owner's name reads 'LOAD 12 TONS'. *courtesy HMRS, AAR202*

CRYNANT COLLIERY Co.

THE colliery was a small anthracite producer with two pits located between Crynant and Seven Sisters stations on the former Neath and Brecon Railway a short distance north of Neath, which could be considered handy for dispatch of some of its limited production of just over 1,000 tons a week, around 125 wagon loads, to Midlands or Lancashire markets. Its offices were located originally at 12 Castle Street, Brecon and later moved to 113 Bute Street, Cardiff.

First wagon orders placed with the Gloucester company were in 1892, when ten new wagons were ordered and a further ten secondhand purchased. A further order was placed in February 1901 for twenty new wagons, followed by a further twenty in August of that year.

For many years the chairman of the colliery company was one J. A. Jebb, also a coal factor and merchant who operated a fleet of around 200 wagons in his own livery. Jebb continued in this position until shortly before his death in 1914. Fifty-four of Jebb's wagons were then sold to A. S. Williams of Bargoed for £35 each. It is obvious that the colliery had many other wagons apart from those purchased from Gloucester as a record of payments for a single month in 1915 shows that £280 2s. 4d. was paid to the British Wagon Company for wagon hire. The same record also shows that £927 2s. 11d. was paid to the Neath & Brecon Railway; £29 13s. 8d. to the Port Talbot Railway; £65 8s. 0d. to the Great Western; £3 1s. 5d. to the Barry Railway; and £5 16s. 1d. to the Rhondda and Swansea Bay Railway for tonnage dues.

In the 1920s the colliery encountered financial difficulties and operated at a loss for several years, many attempts being made to sell it as a going concern. Part of the economic troubles appear to originate with the sinking of a new colliery named Mountain, which was opened in 1916 and was rhetorically a millstone around the company's neck thereafter. In 1926 fifty wagons were hired from the Lincoln Engine & Wagon Company after several of the older wagons had been withdrawn from service and others awaiting repair would not be accepted by the repair contractors owing to outstanding debts. In 1928 a re-financing arrangement was made with the North Central and British Wagon companies for the 210 and 80 wagons on hire respectively but a year later the company went into voluntary liquidation and a scheme of re-organisation brought into being a new management with two directors from Gueret, Llewellyn & Merrett heading the board.

On March 31st 1929 the 290 wagons owned or rented by the Crynant Colliery Company were taken over by Gueret Llewellyn & Merrett, who would in future supply whatever wagons the company needed from their large and fast-expanding fleet. That the 290 wagons are recorded already as being on hire suggests that the new wagons purchased from Gloucester as illustrated had already been disposed of.

The company was operated as a separate entity but was never really successful, lifting only 70,000 tons of coal a year. Kirkham Bros of Swansea were the original sole sales agents, but after the 1929 re-organisation even the might of Gueret, Llewellyn

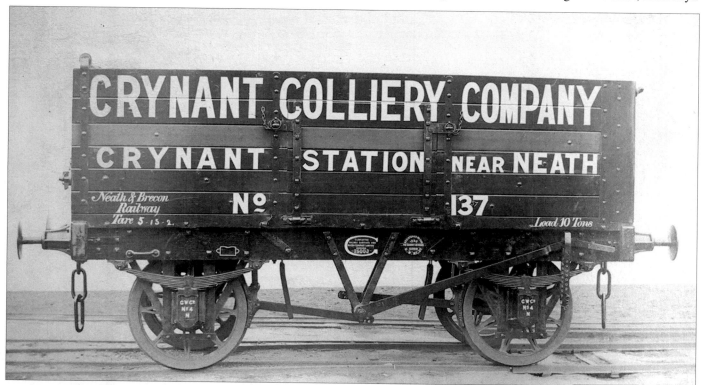

Illustrated are three different wagons from the sequence supplied over several years by the Gloucester company. The oldest is No. 137 from an order for ten wagons supplied in 1892, with six planks, side and end doors, inside diagonal bracing and, inevitably, brakes on one side only. It measured 14ft 6in. x 7ft 3in. x 3ft 5in. internally and was painted black with the third plank from the top red, white unshaded lettering. In italics at bottom left-hand corner 'Neath & Brecon Railway'. The wagon carries a Gloucester owner's plate, No. 25003 and was registered by the GWR.

GRC&WCo.

& Merrett was incapable of its salvation and the company was wound up in 1945 and the collieries closed.

As there are no trading records, the distribution of its coal cannot be determined with any certainty, but looking at the spread of payments to the various railway companies, it is obvious that the Neath & Brecon carried most of it, but it does not say if it went to the docks or inland.

MODELS : None

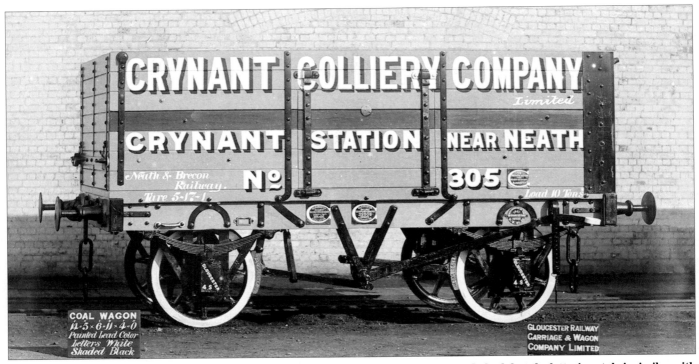

The second wagon, No. 305, shows a change of body colour to 'lead colour' still with the red plank but the lettering style is similar with the addition of black shading and with the word 'Limited' appended in a very amateurish way on the second plank down. It has seven planks and side and end doors, inside diagonal bracing and is from an order placed in September 1901 for 20 wagons. Internal measurements were 14ft 5in. x 6ft 11in. x 4ft 0in. The wagon carries the full range of Gloucester plates, owner's number being 35209 and again registration was with the GWR. *GRC&WCo.*

The third wagon, No. 330, is part of an order for twenty wagons placed in July 1902. It is identical to No. 305 except that the word '*Limited*' is now shaded and executed in a much more professional manner. The Gloucester owner's number is 28277. *GRC&WCo.*

This sequence of four photographs of wagons built by the same maker over a period of less than eight years shows decisions that refer to changes in wagon lettering were made frequently, and more likely with smaller users than the big ones. The oldest wagon is No. 66, delivered in 1900 with seven planks, side and end doors and inside diagonal bracing. It has internal dimensions of 14ft 5in. x 6ft 11in. x 4ft 0in. and was painted black with white letters shaded red. Small italics to left read: '*Empty to Brynamman, Midland Railway, Swansea Valley.*' and at right '*Agents– Letricheux & David, Swansea.*'.
GRC&WCo.

CWMTEG ANTHRACITE COLLIERY Co Ltd

CWMTEG was another of the many small anthracite producers in the Swansea Valley, the colliery being located near Brynamman, terminus of the Midland Railway and interchange point with the Great Western branch from Pantyffynnon. The Cwmteg Colliery was also short lived, it appears to have worked only between 1899 and 1916. The company also owned the Noyadd Colliery at Garnant, further down the Great Western's Pantyffynnon Branch. This was equally short lived and both collieries were closed by 1923.

Two orders for wagons were placed with the Western Wagon Co. of Bristol in 1900, both for twenty 10-ton wagons paid for over 10 years. The second batch of these were built by the Darlington Wagon Co. Cwmteg also placed several orders with the Gloucester company for new wagons between 1900 and 1908 and also purchased two lots that were secondhand:

12.12.1900	30 10-ton new
09.07.1902	50 10-ton new
12.11.1902	40 10-ton new
13.05.1903	50 10-ton new*
09.05.1907	135 10-ton secondhand
11.12.1907	15 10-ton secondhand

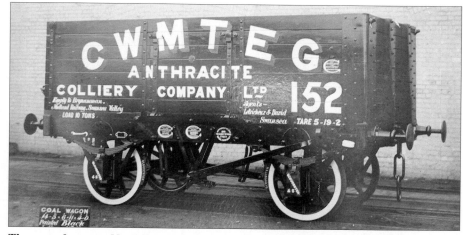

The second wagon, No. 152, was photographed in January 1901 and the lettering style and body colour are identical, with the exception that the curved 'CWMTEG' is much more pronounced and the letter 'G' thereof is totally out of alignment. Dimensions and livery as above.
GRC&WCo.

03.07.1908	20 12 ton new No's 216-235.
	Reg. Midland Rly 58153-58172.

* 25 of these wagons were numbered 201 to 225 and registered with the Midland Railway (Reg. No's 41575 to 41599). A note in the Gloucester records suggests that they were returned and resold to the Cynon Colliery Co., hence the partial duplication of wagon numbers.

Bearing in mind the very short life of the collieries, the wagons would have only been seen in a limited timespan. Assuming both pits to be closed by 1923, the oldest would have been twenty-three years old at that time, roughly half the life of a coal wagon. Therefore they would have been sold off, either to coal merchants, wagon hire firms or other collieries.

MODELS : None

45

The third wagon, No. 101, appears to be from the July 1902 order for fifty new wagons and shows a pronounced change in style. The Noyadd Colliery at Garnant has been added to the information on the wagon body and the colour has changed. The Swansea agent has also disappeared. The wagon has seven planks, side and end doors and inside diagonals, brakes one side and is registered with the GWR rather than the Midland. Internal measurements were 14ft 5in. x 6ft 11in. x 4ft 0in. Body colour was 'lead' with white letters shaded black and black ironwork. Italic letters at bottom left read *Empty to Garnant, G.W.R.*. Note that the letter 'C' of 'CWMTEG' is out of alignment, as it is on wagon No. 66. *GRC&WCo.*

No. 226 was delivered in 1908 and is from an order for 20 wagons numbered 216 to 235 supplied by Gloucester and registered with the Midland Railway. It is another seven-plank ten-ton wagon with side and end doors but this time with outside diagonal bracing. The dimensions and livery of the wagon are identical to No. 101, noting that, as was usual with Gloucester, the diagonal bracing was not picked out in black. It was not an easy lettering job for the signwriter as this time the 'G' of 'CWMTEG' is out of alignment! Italic letters at bottom left read *Empty to Brynamman, M.R.*. *GRC&WCo.*

DENABY & CADEBY MAIN COLLIERIES Co. Ltd

THE Denaby Main Colliery Co. Limited was registered in March 1868 to operate Denaby Main Colliery sunk by its promotors to tap the Barnsley Bed of steam coal which was struck in 1867. The company also sank the Cadeby Main Colliery a short distance away – a geological fault preventing the entire coal reserves being lifted at a single colliery – where sinking was completed in late 1893. The company now changed its name to the Denaby & Cadeby Main Collieries Co. Ltd which was registered in August 1893.

Denaby and Cadeby collieries were situated between Conisborough and Doncaster on the Great Central line from Sheffield to Doncaster, over which the Midland Railway had running rights, and were also connected to both the Dearne Valley Railway and the Hull & Barnsley, which gave immediate access to seaports on both coasts, the industrialised Midlands, Lancashire and Yorkshire, as well as London markets. Both collieries were prolific producers, between them in 1931 output reached 1.8 million tons of household, steam, gas and coking coal which was widely distributed inland and by 1913 over a million tons a year was being transported to Hull for export and bunkering. This is a staggering statistic on its own and accounted for much of the collieries output but when it is considered that one out of every six wagons of coal arriving at Hull came from either Denaby or Cadeby the figures are even more impressive, the next largest shipper was the Carlton Collieries Association, whose Grimethorpe and Frickley pits between them could only muster a little over 400,000 tons.

A million tons of coal in the twelve-ton capacity wagons in use in 1912 suggests around 100,000 wagon loads, that is 2,000 wagon loads a week or 330 wagons a day: up to ten trainloads. Even piled high with large Yorkshire coal they only held an average of ten tons. These figures are for Hull alone, coal was also shipped at the other Humber ports. The sometimes maligned Hull & Barnsley Railway was a very handy link to the port, as it was a direct route.

The Denaby Colliery produced only a limited amount of gas coal, which at the Birmingham Gas Works received the accolade that it was the best coal that they bought. Other gas works supplied were Yeovil, Manchester, Harrogate, Coventry, Cleethorpes and Royston. But it was in the field of steam coal that the colliery was renowned, much being exported, particularly to South America. Large quantities were sent to Hull for onforwarding by sea to the coaling station at Tilbury owned by Hull, Blyth & Co., who were also the Denaby agent in Liverpool where contracts were held for the supply of coal to several steamship lines. The Cardiff coal exporting firm of Evans, Reid & Co. were responsible for sales of Yorkshire coal as well as that from South Wales. Often these shipments were a mixture from several collieries, a contract to supply coal to Montevideo Electricity in Uruguay for a 66,000 ton shipment in ten shiploads saw coal being obtained from Denaby, Cadeby, Maltby, Houghton Main, Rossington, Dinnington, Brodsworth, Bullcroft, Firbeck Main, Yorkshire Main, Markham Main and Hickleton. A strict instruction to all of the collieries was 'MAKE SURE THAT ALL DOCUMENTS SHOW COAL SIZES IN MILLIMETRES AND NOT INCHES!' with a conversion chart for their guidance. A 1934 contract for 150,000 tons from Denaby alone shows the same directions.

The first known wagons were obtained in 1892, when 200 were supplied by the Wakefield Rolling Stock Company, and from whom a locomotive was purchased several years later when that company went into liquidation. Between 1895 and 1902, a large order, numbered from 3755 to 5328 was supplied by Harrison & Camm of Rotherham. A major re-equipment programme was in full swing in the 1930s, Charles Roberts alone supplying 140 new wagons in 1930; 950 in 1935; 90 (numbers 3150 to 3239) of which No. 3200 was an all-steel 12-tonner, and 50 twenty-ton all steel wagons (No's 3246-3295) in 1936 and another 650 (No's 3346 to 3995) in 1937. A further fifty (No's 2600 to 2649) were also supplied in that year by the Derbyshire C&WCo. of Chesterfield. The Midland RC&WCo. had also supplied 300 12-ton wagons in 1935. Eighteen wagons were built in the colliery company shops in 1938. The wagon fleet was constantly being updated right up

No. 6136, is a Hurst Nelson product from *circa* 1909 and registered with the Great Northern Railway. Note the unusual side door – only four planks deep, with a single heavy door stop and a metal strip over the four planks above. The tare weight of 7t. 13cwt is painted on, and the capacity (12-tons) is indicated on a metal plate screwed to the solebar. The wagon body was unpainted timber, which was probably treated in some way. It was lettered in black, shaded red, and had black ironwork. A Hurst Nelson advert in July 1910 showed wagon No. 4417.
courtesy HMRS, ABN626

SOLD NOTE—f.o.b.

TELEGRAMS:—
INLAND "DENCADE, STOCK, LONDON."
FOREIGN "DENCADE, LONDON."

TELEPHONE NOS. 3160 ROYAL
3161 "
3162 "
3163 "

The Denaby & Cadeby Main Collieries Limited
5, Fenchurch Street,
London

Denaby Main Colliery looking over the level crossing on the Great Central Railway north-eastwards towards the pit-head and screens. A rake of empty Denaby Main wagons stand in the middle distance. *Ian Pope collection*

Cadeby Colliery with Denaby Main wagons No's 4663, 1864, 2086, 4200, 2087. The wagon at the extreme left cannot be identified but is probably the oldest as it has dumb buffers and a near horizontal brake lever. *Ian Pope collection*

The photograph of wagon No. 900 was taken at Gloucester in 1933 after an overhaul. Judging by its number, it was almost new, as a fresh numbering sequence had commenced in 1931. The other plates, and the registration plate, on the solebar have been painted over, but all are Gloucester plates and a Wagon Repairs plate. One has to admire the standards of the wagons that were being turned out at Gloucester at the time, even those that were in for repairs. The wagon is fitted with side, end and bottom doors, and is of seven plank construction. For such a wagon it has an unusually low tare weight. Painted red with white letters

shaded black and black ironwork bar the diagonal bracing. Italic letters at bottom right read '*Empty to The Denaby & Cadeby Main Collieries, L.M.S. & L.N.E.R^bys.*'. Originally the diagonal ironwork would have most likely been picked out in black also.   *GRC&WCo.*

until wagon pooling and was purchasing new wagons, including the patent slope sided 14-ton type built by Charles Roberts and other 14-ton steel wagons from both Metropolitan (numbers 9001 to 9150) and Roberts (numbers 9151 to 9300). The Bolton Wagon Co. supplied 275 wagons, No's 2325-2599 and these were the last conventional wooden wagons supplied, the last being delivered in October 1939. A 20-ton all-steel wagon supplied by Roberts was numbered 10000.

In 1927 a new company, Yorkshire Amalgamated Collieries, was formed to oversee the formation of Amalgamated Denaby Collieries Limited, which was finalised in 1936. This consisted of five large and modern collieries, Denaby, Cadeby, Maltby, Dinnington and Rossington. Wagon purchases for the entire group were made as early as 1931 under the Denaby name, but the orders were evidently placed by the temporary holding company, as they were identified with the other collieries when they were delivered. An example are those for the Maltby Colliery as detailed in *Private Owner Wagons: A First Collection.*

Yorkshire Amalgamated Collieries functioned as an umbrella body from 1927 until the new company was formed in 1936. It was also shown to have controlled two other collieries, Darton Main and Strafford, which were not included in the present amalgamation.

On local markets, Denaby coal would have been mainly distributed in the industrial areas of Lancashire, Derbyshire and Yorkshire but some small coal and slack went to power stations in the London area.

The distribution of Denaby wagons would have been as shown above, with the Midland, Great Northern and Great Central lines into London being common haunts. The two kits and transfers relate to two totally different types of wagon, the transfer for the slope sided wagon should be used on model railways depicting the late 1930s only and it should be borne in mind that these were not initially pooled in 1939.

MODELS : Powsides

A lineup of wagons built by Charles Roberts. Those numbers that can be deciphered are from front: 2848, 2818 and 2817. The wagons were painted red body with white letters shaded black and black ironwork.
courtesy HMRS, AAS406

The different wagons shown here represent the progress of the company's fleet between 1900 and 1915. All were built by the Gloucester RC&WCo., who built a large number of new wagons for the company over this period. The oldest, No. 466, photographed in October 1900 is possibly from the first batch of 30 ordered in March. However, against this is the fact that in the Gloucester books the order is shown as being on 10 years deferred purchase and this wagon does not carry a Gloucester owner's plate. It could be a wagon from the second batch of 20 wagons for which an order is dated November as these were paid for in cash and thus no Gloucester owner's plate would be carried. The wagon was painted black with plain white letters and had internal measurements of 14ft 5in. x 6ft 11in. x 4ft 0in. The italic lettering at bottom right reads '*Empty to Duffryn Rhondda Colliery Cymmer, R.S.B.Rᵞ. Advise repairs to Cardiff & South Wales Wagon Co. Ld Tymaen Siding, Cwmavon. R&S.B. Rᵞ*'. The repair instruction is interesting as if the wagon was from the second batch then Gloucester were contracted to do the repairs! It is not easy trying to work out a wagon's history from a photograph.   *GRC&WCo.*

DUFFRYN RHONDDA COLLIERY Co. Ltd

THE Duffryn Rhondda Colliery was located at Cymmer, on the Rhondda & Swansea Bay Railway. Its first management meeting was held on June 16th 1900, concurrent with wagon purchases from the Gloucester RC&WCo. The company went into receivership in 1915, and was almost immediately purchased by the Imperial Navigation Company as a going concern. A note in the contemporary minute book was that the receivers included in the inventory of plant and equipment 25 wagons which belonged to the British Wagon Company, who immediately commenced legal proceedings for their return.

The colliery produced steam coal, the identity of its owners suggesting that it was sold mainly for steamships use, and was producing some 350 to 400 thousand tons of coal a year from what were called No. 1 pit, No. 1 colliery and No.2 colliery.

In 1926 No. 2 colliery was closed for coal winding but remained as a pumping station. In 1918 the most prominent name in the Welsh coal industry, Sir David Llewellyn, was appointed a director, followed in 1928 by Seymour Berry, who also appears in the directorates of many companies directly or indirectly connected with the trade, giving a strong indication of the future of the pits. In 1929 Imperial Navigation itself was placed in voluntary liquidation and a new company, Duffryn Rhondda (1929) Limited was formed. Its directors included not only Sir David Llewellyn, but also H. H. Merrett, already well known for his involvement with many Welsh colliery companies and a fellow partner in Gueret, Llewellyn and Merrett, one of

the largest colliery agents and coal factors and distributors in the country. In the following year it became part of Welsh Associated Collieries Limited, which in turn was liquidated along with several other coal mining firms and together they became part of the enlarged Powell Duffryn group. The Imperial Navigation Company were also major shareholders in Norths Navigation Collieries Ltd, which also ended up as part of Powell Duffryn.

By 1931 production had been reduced to 250,000 tons a year, but under the new management increased to 400,000 tons in 1937.

Under the ownership of the Duffryn Rhondda company between 1900 and 1909, 1,140 wagons were ordered from the Gloucester company alone as detailed below:

14.03.1900	30 new 10-ton, 10 years deferred purchase
14.11.1900	20 new 10-ton, cash plus repairs for 7 years
09.03.1904	25 secondhand 10-ton, 7 years deferred payment plus repairs for 7 years
12.10.1904	repairs 10 years on a total of 45 10-ton wagons
08.02.1905	25 secondhand 10-ton, 9 years deferred payment
08.11.1905	200 new 10-ton, paid for in cash at £60 10s. each
13.11.1907	440 new 12-ton, 10 years deferred purchase, plus repairs for 10 years on a further 25 10-ton wagons
13.05.1908	50 12-ton new, 10 years deferred payment
14.04.1909	200 new 12-ton
08.12.1909	200 new 12-ton

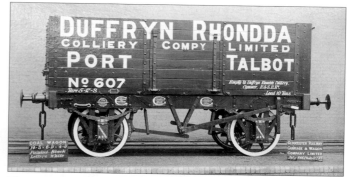

No. 487, probably from the November order for a further 20 wagons, had the same dimensions as No. 466 and the same lettering layout but with only 'Empty to' instructions as in this case a repair contract was signed with Gloucester for a seven year period. The wagon thus carries a Gloucester repairs plate. *GRC&WCo.*

Photographed in July 1906 No. 607 does not appear to fit with any order on the Gloucester books and also shows a change in the lettering layout, 'Duffryn Rhondda' being spread across the top two planks and 'Colliery Compy Limited' added below. It could have been a wagon from the order placed in November 1905 for 200 wagons but they were paid for in cash and this wagon carries a Gloucester owner's plate suggesting that it was on deferred purchase. *GRC&WCo.*

Photographed in April 1907 this wagon again throws up more questions. Once more no order can be found to tie in with the photo unless it is part of the 440 12-ton wagons for which an order was reported in the following November. Notice also that the wagon had external diagonal bracing. *GRC&WCo.*

No. 845, from the 1907 order for 440 wagons, is a very early example of the simplified (and cheaper) livery which shows the initials of the owning company only. This was to be seen on Welsh wagons far more than in any other part of the country. The wagon has seven planks, side and end doors and brakes one side only. The wagon measures internally 15ft 6in. x 7ft 4in. x 4ft 0in. and was painted black with plain white letters as were No's 487, 607 and 698. Italic lettering at bottom left reads 'Empty to Duffryn Rhondda Colliery, Cymmer, R & S. B. Ry.'. *GRC&WCo.*

No. 1002, delivered in 1908, shows a variation to the previous wagon. The running number has been moved to above the door, and the body colour altered. The livery this time is a 'chocolate body', white letters shaded black, and black vertical ironwork. Again it was a seven-plank wagon with side and end doors and brakes one side only. It had slightly larger dimensions, those being 16ft 0in. x 7ft 4in. x 4ft 0in. The italic empty instructions are as the other wagons. The colour chocolate was used with reasonable frequency by Gloucester RC&WCo. and it has been interpreted to mean the colour of dark chocolate. However, it has been subject to various modelled interpretations from black to the colour of a popular brand of milk chocolate made in Birmingham. *GRC&WCo.*

Two further wagons, No's 1107 and 1175 photographed in July 1909 and August 1911 respectively. Both were black with plain white lettering.
GRC&WCo.

Also there must have been a further 50 10-ton wagons on which repair contracts were signed whose origins are unknown.

To this can be added a further 100 ordered by the Imperial Navigation Company in 1915. These wagons were considered not long after they were delivered as excess to requirements and initially disposal was anticipated but in October of that year this was wisely deferred. In June 1919, the company decided immediately to have the second set of brakes fitted to its entire wagon fleet, and the first 320 were converted by the Cambrian Wagon Company at a cost of £9 11s. 2d. each.

The very much simplified livery of initials only dates back to 1907, and is possibly the first application of such, which was to become common in later years. Of the numerous surviving builders' photographs, wagon No. 845 built in that year is the lowest numbered wagon to bear simply the initials 'D R' and it is likely that the older wagons were repainted accordingly when they came in for repainting. Following the takeover by Welsh Associated Collieries, these would have probably disappeared by 1935 to emerge eventually in the very simple Powell Duffryn livery of 'P D' in white letters on a black body.

The sales agents for the colliery were Lysbergs of Cardiff, another company in which the names of Llewellyn, Merrett and Berry appear as directors. The company had extensive connections in France and this is where much of the exported Duffryn Rhondda coal would have been sent to. Lysberg Limited were also represented at Hull, London and Newcastle and it is possible that the wagons could also have been sent to those ports.

MODELS : None.

The final wagon, No 1259, is from the 1915 order placed by the Imperial Navigation Company, but still sports the Duffryn Rhondda livery. It was a 12-ton wagon with side and end doors and brakes on both sides. The changes from the lettering of the previous wagon are simple, the empty return instructions and the wagon number have exchanged places. The livery remained the same – black body and white letters. The empty return instructions were also as before.
GRC&WCo.

The solitary known wagon belonging to this partnership was purchased new from Gloucester in July 1915, on seven years deferred purchase terms, and registered with the LNWR. It had six normal planks plus an unusually narrow plank at the top, side doors only with a lift-over hinged door, brakes on both sides and inside diagonal bracing. It measured internally 15ft 6in. x 7ft 0in. x 4ft 0in. and was smartly finished with a red body, white letters shaded black and black ironwork.   *GRC&WCo.*

EALES & ROBERTS

THE small village of Long Buckby, Northamptonshire, was for many decades recognised as the home of the traditional ornamental water can carried by the narrow boats plying Britain's internal waterway system. This was for many years, and in some parts may still be, referred to as a 'Long Buckby Can'. The association between the village, the Grand Union Canal and coal traffic is an indelible one, canals were built to serve the collieries between Coventry and Nuneaton in the eighteenth century, and coal was the major traffic southbound on the canal. In the early records of the Wyken Colliery held in Coventry archives, is a scrawled letter to the colliery dating back to the days before the railway was even thought of "Send me another boatload of your best cobbles to Long Buckby Wharf' which shows that before the LNWR came the trading heart of Long Buckby was the canal. The most likely way that the order was sent to the colliery was not by mail, but given to the skipper of a canal boat which was going to the colliery to load.

The village, some distance from the canal wharf itself, is notable today more for its proximity to Althorp, the celebrated seat of the Spencer family, than for its canal connections, or for the fact that its railway station has survived the series of hatchets that have been wielded through the railway network and is now served by a regular electrified commuter service to and from London.

Long Buckby Station is located on the former London & North Western secondary line from Rugby to Northampton and the firm of Eales & Roberts were trading there as early as 1905. They still had a wagon in 1933 and were at West Street in 1939. Coal supplies would have almost certainly originated from the Nuneaton or Coventry area via the former LNWR line, and the wagon illustrated would not have strayed far from this particular area.

MODELS : None

ECKERSLEY BROS

ECKERSLEY Bros were a long established concern in the Staffordshire market town of Uttoxeter, on the North Staffordshire Railway's line from Stoke-on-Trent to Derby. Their office address was William Deacons Bank Chambers, and the physical side of the business was conducted from The Coal Wharf at Uttoxeter Station.

The company traded mainly with the nearby North Staffordshire collieries, and also held a regular contract with the Churnet Valley Gas Co. at Frognall, supplying 1,000 tons of gas coal a year from the Madeley Colliery at Leycett. The companys wagons also traded to the Foxfield Colliery near Cheadle and the Sneyd Colliery at Burslem.

In 1924 the company placed an order with the Midland Railway Carriage & Wagon Co. for five 12-ton coal wagons numbered 44 to 47 which were registered in February by the LMS (No's 90934-37). Another batch were numbered 60-64, one of which is illustrated overleaf.

Being coal factors, it is possible that their wagons may have travelled over a wide area of Staffordshire and possibly penetrating into adjoining counties, supplying smaller coal merchants who did not own their own wagons. Once again it is the lack of records that denies us of such knowledge.

MODELS : None

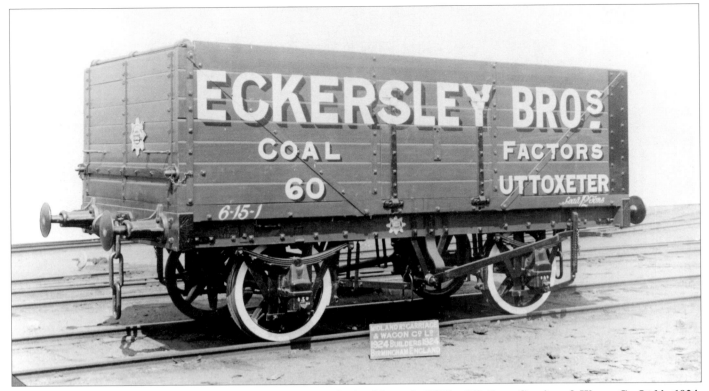

The wagon illustrated is one of five side and end door vehicles obtained from the Midland Railway Carriage & Wagon Co. Ltd in 1924, numbered 60 to 64 and registered with the LMS. The registers state they were fitted with steel underframes and brakes on both sides. Internal dimensions were 16ft 1in. x 7ft 7in. x 4ft 4in. The wagon appears to be painted a medium grey with white letters shaded black. Black ironwork only on door hinge straps, corner plates and the horizontal strapping bar on the end door. Note also the MRC&WCo. owner's plate on the end door.

Birmingham Central Library

ELDERS NAVIGATION COLLIERIES Ltd

THIS is another example of a steamship company becoming a colliery owner with the intention of supplying its own ships on its regular line services to the Canary Islands and the British colonies on the west coast of Africa, bringing mostly palm oil – for the soapmaking and food trade – and fruit back to the British Isles, with general cargo in the opposite direction.

The Elder Dempster Steam Navigation Company was established in 1852 and following the acquisition of the competing Palm Line and other smaller concerns, eventually owned a fleet of 105 ships. The company fell on hard times in the 1920s and eventually folded up. From the ruins a new company was formed in 1932, which traded for many years until the advent of containerisation of cargoes which changed the face of the industry forever, including the disappearance of many of the great names of shipping companies which had become household words throughout the world. The Elder Dempster company eventually became part of the Ocean Transport & Trading group, into which had been merged many familiar names in the industry, including Wm. Cory & Sons, one of the biggest in the coal shipping, trading, bunkering and transporting business. Cory Bros (a different Cory) were also the sales agents for the colliery, and that Elders coal was sold on the open market in Southampton is an indication that the steamship company did not use all of it.

Elders Navigation Collieries Limited were the owners of the Oakwood Colliery, a short distance south of Maesteg on the Great Western Railway branch from Tondu to Maesteg and the Llynfi Valley. Oakwood was purchased by the company circa 1900, and then passed on to the Celtic Oakwood Collieries Company shortly before it was worked out roughly 25 years later. It is impossible to prove that the wagons owned by and lettered 'CELTIC' were acquired at the same time, but Celtic wagons were certainly around in the late 1920s. At around the same time the company also owned another colliery, Garth Merthyr, near Garth on the Port Talbot Railway, which was a convenient location as this railway was owned by the same interests as the docks at Port Talbot. This also ended up in the ownership of Celtic Collieries Limited.

That the company decided to retire from the colliery business in the 1920s is concurrent with the more general introduction of liquid fuel: in 1925 they had a known contract for the purchase of fuel oil which is an indication of the change in fuels which indirectly was responsible for the decline in both the production and sale of high quality steam coal, for which South Wales was famous.

The company purchased new wagons from both Hurst Nelson and the Gloucester company, the solitary model of an Elders Navigation wagon was a limited edition based on the latter and its presence on model railways should be limited to those depicting a period 1905 to 1925 and in the area around Port Talbot and the collieries, although coal may have been carried

The wagon illustrated is from an order for 25 placed with the Gloucester RC&WCo. in 1900. It had seven planks, side and end doors, brakes one side and internal diagonal bracing. Internal measurements were 14ft 6in. x 6ft 11in. x 4ft 0in. The wagon was painted black with white letters unshaded. Italic letters at bottom left read: '*Empty to Oakwood Siding Maesteg, G.W.R*ʸ.'. Some wagons, built by Hurst Nelson, had different instructions: '*Empty to Cwmdu Sidings, for repairs return to Colliery, Maesteg*' and in contradiction at the other end '*Repairs advise North Central Wagon Co, Cardiff.*'. *GRC&WCo.*

in them to other ports where Elder Dempster ships traded, we have no evidence of this, although it is known that the ships worked into Liverpool and Southampton regularly. It is also known that occasionally wagon loads of Welsh steam coal and anthracite appeared at such east coast ports as Hull, obviously railed direct to a regular local client whose ships had visited that port for some specific reason. Quantities varied from a

couple of wagon loads to a consignment of 277 tons from Cwmgorse. Elders also purchased Yorkshire coal from Bullcroft Main in the early 20th century.

MODELS : Dapol/Whyborn

Three Elders wagons, all bearing variations in the livery applied. *courtesy National Museums & Galleries of Wales*

A stunning picture postcard view of the Garth Merthyr Colliery in the Llynfi Valley containing much of interest – from the proud display of the owner's name on the side of the screens building to the number and variety of wagons in the sidings. Many of these are coke wagons and the bank of coke ovens can be seen to the left in the middle distance. Notice that several of the coke wagons are sheeted over with tarpaulins bearing the wording 'Elders Navigation Specially Selected Foundry Coke'. This would have been carefully screened, loaded into the wagons and then covered to keep it dry in transit – not many foundries would have wanted to waste energy in drying the coke in their forges and furnaces before getting any real heat from it. Most of the wagons identifiable belong to Elders, some branded for Maesteg, others for Cardiff. In the line closest to the camera are a 6-plank coke wagon, No. 506 branded Cardiff; what could be a 5-plank with side and end doors and external diagonal strapping, No. 407 for Maesteg; a 4-plank dumb-buffered No. 125 for Maesteg; No. 422, possibly 6-plank with side and end doors and a completely different lettering layout with Maesteg to the right; No. 69 lettered for Maesteg; then four sheeted coke wagons No's 277 (lettered for Maesteg), 535, 515 and 584 for Cardiff; finally 665 and 813 both again displaying differences in lettering styles. In the rows behind coke wagons No's 587 and 518, and coal wagons No's 341 and 713 can be identified. Emerging from the screens are two wagons for A. E. T. Richards, Traffic Agent, Tondu, numbered 4 and 5, the latter being dumb-buffered. Albert Richards is known to have taken two wagons from Gloucester in 1899, one of which was numbered 2. Photographs of this nature show how little has been recorded of many fleets. *Neil Parkhouse collection*

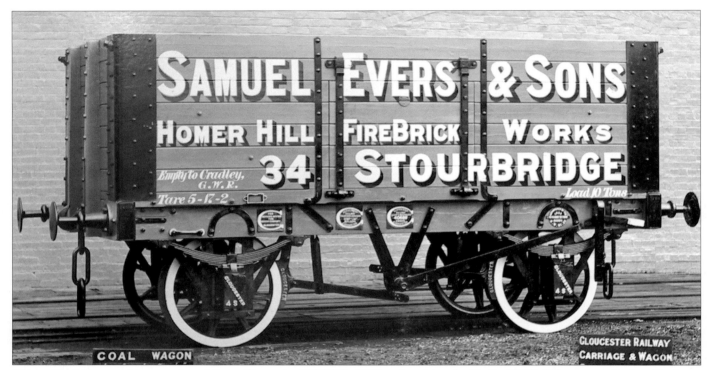

Wagon No. 34 is one of two purchased from Gloucester RC&W in 1903 and registered with the GWR. It has seven planks, side doors only, inside diagonal bracing and brakes one side. Its internal dimensions are 14ft 5in. x 6ft 11in. x 4ft 0in. and it was painted dark lead with white letters shaded red and with black vertical ironwork. In italics at bottom left: *'Empty to Cradley, G.W.R.'*.   *GRC&WCo.*

SAMUEL EVERS & SONS

THE company was the owner of the Homer Hill Firebrick Works at Cradley, on the Great Western's Stourbridge Extension Line in the heart of the Black Country, albeit Stourbridge was shown on its wagon sides. It later became a subsidiary of E. & J. Pearson Ltd, itself a large manufacturer of firebricks based at Amblecote, near Stourbridge, and owners of five fireclay mines at Amblecote and Brierley Hill.

Firebricks are a specific type manufactured from fireclay and differ from standard bricks in that they are far more resistant to high temperatures as encountered in furnaces, kilns, chimney bases, ovens etc. It is obvious that fireclay was found in large quantities in the Stourbridge area as there were no less than eight different makers who owned brickworks. Some, like Samuel Evers, also mined coal where there were seams nearby similar to those at Swadlincote, and this was used at the brickworks, the company mining some 12,000 tons per annum although the brickworks outlived the colliery.

The only wagons known to have been owned by the company were the two purchased from Gloucester in 1903 and maintained by them through to at least 1924 although in 1918 the repair contract would have been taken over by Wagon Repairs Ltd. Although these were standard coal wagons they may also have been used to transport bricks, although the most suitable wagons for such loads were either five-plank with full height doors or those with full length drop sides for ease of loading and unloading. The distribution of firebricks could have been widespread, depending on local demand and availability.

MODELS : Cambrian/Whyborn

EVESONS (COAL) Ltd

ONE of the giants of the coal trade of the Midlands, Evesons were based in Birmingham with a very busy and important office in Barnsley as well as a branch in Belfast, which, although not advertised, suggests that they also shipped coal across the Irish Sea. There were several other Evesons in the coal trade and the family association with the industry is a long standing one, Evesons were trading at Birmingham and Stourbridge as early as the 1860s.

In 1925 there were Evesons trading at Kidderminster, (Eveson & Co.) Stourbridge, (Evesons Coals and G. J. Eveson) Bridgnorth (Evesons Coal & Coke) and Birmingham (Evesons Coals). It has not been possible to determine if this is the one and same business trading under different names for contractual reasons, but what had appeared by 1938 were:

Evesons (Coal) Ltd	7 Eastgate, Barnsley; 142 Royal Avenue, Belfast; 134 Edmund Street, Birmingham; and Hollybush Road, Bridgnorth
Evesons (Coal) Ltd	High St, Stourbridge
Eveson & Co. Ltd	1 High St, Stourbridge
Noel Eveson Ltd	Monument Lane, Birmingham

The company was the principal sales agent for the Wath Main Colliery (see page 107) and supplied gas coal over a very large area of the country. It was also sales agent for the Hatfield Main Colliery for a large part of Yorkshire and for Warwickshire, and for the Dearne Valley Colliery for part of Yorkshire.

Evesons wagons could have been seen at almost every colliery in the Warwickshire coalfield and at those of Leicestershire and South Derbyshire, in particular at Donisthorpe, where forty wagons were recorded in one week. The company also patronised Highley Colliery near Kidderminster and Madeley

Wood Colliery in Shropshire; Clifton, Bentinck, New Hucknall, Annesley and Welbeck in Notts; Clay Cross and Shipley in Derbyshire as well as Sneyd and Foxbridge in North Staffordshire and others in that county. Gas coal was also sold from Bersham in North Wales; Cortonwood, Wombwell, Aldwarke Main and Flockton in Yorkshire and Glapwell, Ireland and Markham Main in Derbyshire. From Hatfield Main Colliery, Evesons wagons were despatched to Heckmondwicke, Brightside (Sheffield), Shipley, Armley, Dewsbury, Holyhead, Brighouse, Holmfirth, Lightcliffe (Sheffield) and Stratford-on-Avon in one month, and from Dearne Valley to Glossop, Hadfield, Broadbottom and Mottram (Manchester).

However, this is nothing compared with distribution from Wath Main, where Evesons negotiated gas coal contracts for the following gas works: Oldbury, Stony Stratford, Coalville, Mossley, Saddleworth, Rowley Regis, Buxton, Wallasey, Solihull, Alcester, Wolverhampton, Willenhall, Banbury, Melbourne, Bradford, Gloucester, Rugby, Leicester, Rushton, Saffron Waldon, Clacton, Rothwell, Lea Bridge, Swindon (GWR), Shoeburyness, Raunds, Narborough, Market Harborough, Scunthorpe, Kidderminster, Tipton, Halesowen, Knowle and Dorridge, Bromsgrove, Stow-on-the-Wold, Worcester, Sandbach, Chelmsford, Oswaldtwistle, Nelson, Stroud, Hinckley, Sandy, Sleaford, Henley-in-Arden, Oakham and St. Neots.

This may seem a long roll-call, but the total amount supplied was in the vicinity of 100,000 tons per annum, which is only a third of what Wilson Carter & Pearson supplied to the City of Birmingham alone. Nevertheless, it indicates what a substantial force Evesons were (and are, as the company is still in business as suppliers of liquid fuel) for this constituted only a percentage of their trade: they also dealt with collieries that supplied both household and industrial coal and their clientele in this field would have been just as substantial but possibly not as widespread.

Therefore Evesons wagons could have been seen in most parts of the country, the fleet was a large one although few details of it have emerged. The company also built railway wagons at their Albion Wagon Works, not only for their own fleet – ten 12-ton wagons were built between 1927 and 1929 and numbered 6500-5, 6508 and 6511-5 – but also for general sale.

The company, in 1937-38, purchased a large fleet of 188 12-ton capacity wagons from Hurst Nelson Ltd which were sold, shortly before nationalisation, to the Gloucester RC&WCo. for £180 each. These wagons were financed by the North Central Wagon Company and registered with the LMS. They were numbered 7001 to 7562 in threes, i.e. 7001, 7004, 7007, 7010 etc. In the Gloucester minutes which refer to their purchase, it is recorded that the wagons were built by Bell of Doncaster. This company went out of business in 1929, unexpectedly the wagon company's records are incorrect in this instance.

MODELS : Dapol/Midlander

The illustration of the Eveson wagon taken from the unbraked side shows just how crude and flimsy these vehicles appeared to be when photographed as such. Taken at Blackwell (assumed as the Blackwell at the top of the Lickey Incline), it is loaded with huge lumps of hand picked best coal which was probably destined for a large country house. Eveson's wagons were red with white letters.
courtesy Roger Carpenter

FRANKLIN & SON

Based on the information passed on down the years with the photograph, reproduced from a much larger framed print, the location is believed to be the wagon repair works of Thomas Moy at Peterborough. The date is unknown but all four wagons have the second set of brakes fitted. The design suggests that they were not new wagons, despite the consecutive numbers, but were wagons supplied either secondhand or older wagons of the company which had come in for repair and overhaul. It is therefore suggested that the date of the photograph is from the period when the company name was as shown, between 1903 and 1910. The wagons were painted red with white lettering shaded black and black ironwork.   *Colin Underwood collection*

THIS was a very old established company and one of many Franklins trading in coal and general merchandise in Hertfordshire and Bedfordshire, although what family relations exist is undetermined. Apart from Henry Franklin of Biggleswade there was in 1895 a T. Franklin at Hitchin, Knebworth and Stevenage, and later a T. W. & P. Franklin at Baldock, Hitchin, Knebworth and Stevenage, which was listed from 1910 to 1935 and another company called Franklin, Bryden (1935) Ltd. Any family relationship with Charles Franklin of Bedford, one of the biggest coal merchants in the general area, is unknown.

Henry Franklin of Biggleswade was a coal merchant at the local railway station on the former Great Northern Railway east coast main line as early as 1864. In 1869 the business was shown as operated by Mrs. Henry Franklin, apparently after her husband had died and by 1879 the ownership reverted to Henry Franklin, probably a son who had taken over. It is known that in 1881 Henry was living in Station Road, Biggleswade, and, aged 30, was a coal merchant.

By 1898 the company had expanded into water and steam milling and the marketing of coal, corn, coke, salt, manure, hay, straw and soot. The company was also an agent for the Westminster Fire Office and Mutual Insurance, with depots at Arlesley, Biggleswade and Hitchin. By 1910 the notation '& Son' had been added to the trading name, which was maintained until 1928 when the title reverted to Henry Franklin, who may

have been the grandson of the original Henry Franklin. By 1936 a limited company had been formed. A 1937 drawing by Wagon Repairs Ltd shows a 'Henry Franklin Ltd' wagon painted red oxide with white letters, shaded black.

Franklin traded extensively with Nottingham and Derbyshire collieries, regularly purchasing Welbeck hard steam coal from the New Hucknall company as well as household coal from Bentinck and Annesley. Coal was also purchased from the Clifton Colliery near Nottingham, Warsop Main near Mansfield and coke from the Blackwell Colliery near Alfreton. It would be expected that the Yorkshire collieries around Doncaster, with their direct access to each of Franklin's depots via the east coast main line would also have been suppliers.

MODELS : None

Photographed in October 1922 was this seven-plank, side, end and bottom door wagon fitted with brakes both sides. Registered with the Midland (No. 78043) and also carrying a Gloucester owner's plate. Painted lead colour with white lettering shaded black and with black ironwork excluding the external diagonal strapping. *'Empty to South Leicestershire Colliery, Coalville, Via Midland Rly.'. GRC&WCo.*

FULTON & Co. Ltd

THE first references to wagons owned by this company was in September 1922, when 30 secondhand eight-ton wagons were hired from the Gloucester company. This was the start of a 20 year association with this manufacturer for both new, secondhand and hired wagons, although new wagons were also purchased from Wm. Rigley & Co. of Bulwell, Notts; G. R. Turner of Langley Mill and Charles Roberts of Wakefield.

Fulton & Co. Ltd appear to have moved their office about as 3 Cross Lane, Abbey House, Victoria St, SW1, and later 6 Euston Road, London all appear. They were a medium sized coal merchant who, from the outset, preferred smaller wagons, suggesting much of the company's business was in household coal and unloaded in the traditional manner. They were a latecomer to the London scene, commencing business around 1920 with a depot at the coal wharf, and later at St. Pancras Station.

A number of the company's new wagons emptied to the Upton Colliery at North Elmsall and considering that this was one of the last new collieries to open before the outbreak of the second world war, could have been one of the few London coal merchants to have patronised it.

Between 1922 and 1939, Fultons hired or purchased 310 wagons from the Gloucester company alone as follows:

09.1922	30	8-ton hired
09.1922	30	12-ton new No's 200-229, registered Midland 78028-78057
01.1923	20	12-ton new No's 230-249, registered LMS 82857-82876
01.1923	20	12-ton hired
09.1931	20	12-ton secondhand, paid cash £75/10/- each
10.1931	25	10-ton hired
09.1932	30	8-ton hired

A line-up of part of the order for thirty wagons which included No. 215 outside the works at Gloucester. All appear to be branded empty to the same destination.

GRC&WCo.

61

Both of these wagons were obtained from Gloucester in the 1930s, the first when that company was selling off large quantities of ex-rental stock at very enticing prices. No. 602 was sold in 1931 for cash and was a seven-plank wagon with side, end and bottom doors and a fixed top through plank with the cutaway above the door. The registration plate appears to be GWR No. 60539 of 1924. The wagon has a black body with white letters shaded red. Italic letters at bottom left read '*Empty to Upton Colliery, North Elmsall, L&N.E.Rly.*'.

GRC&WCo.

The second wagon, No. 800, is much older. It was delivered in August 1932 and was one of 30 8-ton wagons hired during that month and painted in the customers own colours. The GWR registration plate appears to read No. 1147 of 1896, although it will be noted that the second set of brakes had been fitted, suggesting that the hire was for a lengthy period. The abbreviated livery, when compared with No. 602, was probably applied as there was not enough space on the wagon side for that which adorned its companion! The livery in this instance was a black body with plain white letters. Italic letters at bottom left read '*Empty to Arley Colliery, L.M.S.*'. Arley Colliery was near Nuneaton on the line between Nuneaton and Water Orton in Warwickshire. It was described in *Private Owner Wagons: A First Collection*.

GRC&WCo.

No. 250 was photographed new in September 1939 when ten 13-ton wagons were purchased. Again it had the cutaway above the side door and was also fitted with bottom doors. Empty instructions on the left are to Radford Colliery, L.M.S. Livery has reverted to a black body with white lettering shaded red.
GRC&WCo.

09.1936	25	unknown hired
10.1936	25	12-ton hired
10.1937	10	12-ton new
09.1939	10	13-ton new 250-259 reg. LMS 166458-166467*
10.1939	30	10-ton hire
11.1939	20	12-ton new
08.1942	25	13-ton new 280-294, steel frames, registered in 1943

* These wagons had the cutaway top plank generally known as the London Plank.

No. 250 emptied to the Radford Colliery of the Wollaton Colliery Co, Nottingham.

Wagons known to have been purchased from other suppliers were:

05.1923	25	Turner No's 300-324 registered LMS 87783- 87807
12.1923	14	Turner No's 325-338 registered LMS 88216-88229
1936	25	Rigley No's 500-525
12.1939	15	Rigley No's 526-541 registered LMS 166442-166456
12.1939	20	Roberts No's 260-279 registered LMS 166771-166790

From the above, it can be immediately deduced that the numbering system was quite haphazard and that there was a regular flurry to hire or order wagons in the autumn, which suggests that there was always an upsurge in trade around this time.

Apart from those illustrated, Fulton wagons also emptied to the Staveley and Blackwell collieries in Derbyshire, to the Griff Colliery in Warwickshire and coal was regularly purchased from the Bentinck and Annesley collieries in Nottinghamshire. The livery was later standardised as black, some wagons having red or red oxide shading – the latter was specified to Wagon Repairs Limited of Wellingborough for repainting of the company's wagons in 1936.

MODELS : None

Wagons were supplied to Fulton during the second world war, No's 289 and 300 being photographed in February and March 1943, probably both from the same order placed in August the previous year. They were finished identically in black with white lettering and both were of 13-ton capacity with side, end and bottom doors and were fitted with 3-hole disc wheels. Again the 'empty to' instructions are for Radford Colliery. *GRC&WCo.*

No. 306 was the last of six wagons purchased in 1935 from GRC&WCo., numbered 301 to 306, and registered with the LNER (No's 8863 to 8868.) It had side, end and bottom doors, seven planks and brakes on both sides, with internal dimensions of 16ft 1in. x 7ft 7in. x 4ft 4in. Painted red with black vertical ironwork and white letters shaded black. The italic lettering on the solebar reads '*For Repairs advise C. E. Gardner, Norwich*'. The adjoining oval plate reads '**C. E. GARDNER, OWNER, NORWICH**'. *GRC&WCo.*

C. E. GARDNER

THE coal merchant C. E. Gardner, of 70 Queens Road, Norwich appears to have commenced business around 1927, when he first appears in the Coal Trade Directory listing.

Although having wagons in 1928 his only known purchases of new wagons was from the distant Gloucester company, rather than one of the Nottinghamshire or Derbyshire wagon builders in the coalfields where most coal for the Norwich area originated. In 1935 the Gloucester-built wagons were registered to W. V. & C. E. Gardner but by 1938 it was just C. E. Gardner.

Unfortunately there is no record at which of the three Norwich stations Gardner traded from, coal from pits served by the LMS could have arrived at Norwich City via Melton Mowbray and Melton Constable and the Midland & Great Northern Joint Line, that from the Worksop area – favoured by many East Anglian coal merchants – via Retford, Sleaford and March. Therefore the wagons would have probably only been

Gardner was another merchant who bought new wagons during wartime as witnessed by No. 307 photographed at Gloucester in April 1943. A standard RCH 1923 pattern 8-plank wagon of 13-ton capacity, it is finished in red with plain white lettering and black ironwork excepting the diagonal bracing. The diagonal bracing on the left-hand end has been picked out in white to aid the identification of the end door by wagon tippers during the black-out. The 'Empty to' instructions have been left blank, possibly because the wagon would be going direct into the pool and could therefore have been sent anywhere. *GRC&WCo.*

seen between East Anglia and the Notts and Derbyshire coalfield.

MODELS : None

No. 719 is from an order placed in 1900 with the Gloucester RC&WCo. for 150 wagons and registered with the GWR (the number appears to be 42267) and being bought on deferred purchase it also carries the Gloucester owner's number 35353. It has seven planks, side and end doors, steel underframe and brakes one side. It would appear that this side has the usual circular plate on the door to act as a buffer when the door drops against the brake gear whilst the far side has a steel spring door stop. The wagon has internal dimensions of 14ft 5in. x 6ft 11in. x 4ft 0in. and is painted 'Lead colour' with white letters shaded black and black ironwork – note that this extends to the diagonal bracing, unusual in Gloucester-built wagons. The emblem on the door consists of a white circle, edged black, and a black diamond containing a yellow 'G' and a red cross. Italic letters at bottom left read *'Empty to Gellyceidrim Collieries, Garnant. G.W. R.'*.

GRC&WCo.

GELLYCEIDRIM COLLIERIES Co. Ltd

GELLYCEIDRIM Colliery was situated at Garnant, on the Great Western branch from Glanamman to Brynamman which served numerous anthracite producers and like many, was a comparatively small concern producing an average of 2,000 tons (200 to 250 wagon loads) a week.

It was working at least as early as 1895 and in October 1896 hired 25 wagons from the Gloucester RC&WCo. for a six month period. Fifty were taken on 11 months hire in May 1898 but there is no way of knowing whether this included the original 25. In March 1900 an order was placed for 150 new wagons with Gloucester and a further 96 were hired for 2 years – again this hire was a renewal so may have included the 50 from 1898. By 1901 the company was so far in arrears in its payments that legal action was taken for recovery of amounts owing for almost two years.

In both 1908 and 1918 the colliery employed just over 500 hands and the company had its registered offices at 14 Cambrian Place, Swansea.

In 1923 the company lost its independence and was taken over by Cleeves Western Valley Anthracite Collieries Ltd to become part of the embryo Amalgamated Anthracite company, which eventually incorporated a majority of collieries in this part of Wales.

By 1945 only one of the two pits was working, the other being relegated to a pumping station.

The Gellyceidrim wagons would have been repainted into their new owner's livery by the early 1930s and therefore wagons such as that illustrated would only have been seen over

the period 1900 to that date. Their scope of operation would have been to local seaports for the export trade, and inland to most places where anthracite was used, once again there are no records of this colliery that have survived to tell us where specifically their actual markets were. However, the Cleeves organisation was a substantial one with offices and facilities at major seaports throughout the country, in addition to its own steamship fleet.

MODELS : Bachmann

A postcard view of the colliery at Glanamman which was a drift, or slant, with a journey of pit tubs emerging from under the building. *Pope/Parkhouse Archive*

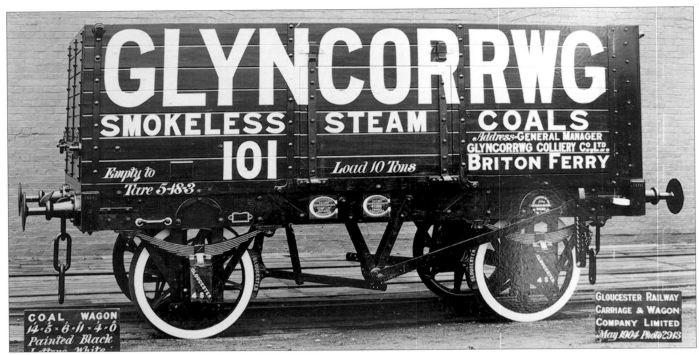

A page of Glyncorrwg wagons built between 1904 and 1907. The photographs are dated May 1904 for No. 101, April 1905 for No. 842, No. 968, March 1906, and May 1907 for No. 1176. The livery has remained consistent, with slight variations in the company title at bottom right. It will be noted that like many Welsh colliery wagons, the registered office of the company is shown on the wagon side rather than the location of the collieries themselves. All of the wagons are of ten tons capacity with side and end doors, inside diagonal bracing and brakes one side only. All have the internal dimensions of 14ft 5in. x 6ft 11in. x 4ft 0in. They are all painted black with white letters unshaded. At the bottom of the page are two of the Gloucester built wagons in service, at Wright Butler & Co's works at Cwmavon. Note the strange effect on the side doors which cannot be explained.

GRC&WCo. and *John Horne collection*

GLYNCORRWG COLLIERY Co. Ltd

MINING at Glyncorrwg, at the far end of the South Wales Mineral Railway and the easternmost limit of the south Wales anthracite beds, was obviously in full swing in 1872 as the Glyncorrwg Colliery commenced hiring wagons from the Gloucester Wagon Co. in that year. In April 150 10-ton wagons were taken on a three year hire. This may have been in connection with the conversion of the broad gauge lines in the area which was undertaken in May as in July a contract was signed with Gloucester for the conversion of broad gauge wagons. The hire of the 150 wagons was renewed in July 1875. Three years later a further hire of 75 wagons was undertaken, but only for three months, and in the easy-going business atmosphere of the time, these were delivered even though the colliery was already behind to the tune of nearly two years on its existing account, which by May 1879 had extended to three years.

References in an 1895 directory show a colliery of this name, as well as a Tunnel Colliery, at Abergwynfi under the ownership of William Perch & Company. The latter is assumed to have been located at the Abergwynfi end of the Rhondda Tunnel, which carried the Rhondda & Swansea Bay Railway from Abergwynfi to Treherbert. William Perch & Company were a very well known name in the Welsh coal trade, owning the Rigos Colliery and acting as sales agents for several others, as well as trading on the international market. The later Glyncorrwg Colliery Company Limited appears to be the subsequent owner of both: Glyncorrwg had closed but was redeveloped and re-opened in 1904, concurrently launching a substantial purchasing programme of new railway wagons, with 600 coming from the Gloucester company alone within three years, four hundred ordered in April 1904, a further two hundred in December 1904, and a hundred each in February and December 1906, all were on 10 year deferred purchase terms. In 1910 the company extended the purchase period on the wagons for a further 10 years.

The Glyncorrwg collieries (there were two) were situated beyond the village of that name on the South Wales Mineral Railway and it is understood that there was a financial connection with the latter. The railway itself reached further into the hills of South Wales to serve the New Rhondda and Bleancorrwg pits at its furthest point. Although again closed betweeen 1912 and 1919, by 1923 Glyncorrwg was obviously thriving as 253,000 tons of coal were raised with a payroll of 1,100 men from this and Blaengynfi collieries, the latter may have been the original Tunnel Colliery.

The collieries produced 'smokeless steam coal' the market for which may have been spread across the country, and although no records exist to show where Glyncorrwg coal was actually sold, the company advertised in trade and commercial newspapers and magazines that related to the shipping of coal from South Wales ports, so it must have exported in quantity.

Therefore it is surprising to find that Glyncorrwg, like several other pits across the country, should suddenly close and its assets sold off, it is recorded that in July 1925 the entire plant was dismantled. The site lay idle for two years until it was acquired by the Vale of Neath Colliery Co., owners of the large mine at Aberpergwm. Production was restored of 'smokeless steam coal'

and the colliery continued to thrive. In 1927 the Vale of Neath company and its several pits was absorbed into Amalgamated Anthracite. In 1950 it was mining anthracite with 772 personnel.

Under the name of Glyncorrwg that company ordered 500 14-ton all steel wagons from Charles Roberts & Co. in March 1943, under the wartime emergency wagon building programme detailed in *Private Owner Wagons: A First Collection*. These were hired from Glyncorrwg Wagons Ltd, a Roberts subsidiary, numbers are believed to have been 33466 to 33965. These were part of a batch of 53 of Robert's patent 14-ton slope-sided all-steel wagons.

The original Glyncorrwg wagons (at least 1,400) were probably all registered with the Great Western. However, when the original plant and equipment were sold off in 1925, it is most likely that they were bought in parcels by another colliery, a large fleet owner or a wagon hire company.

MODELS : Powsides

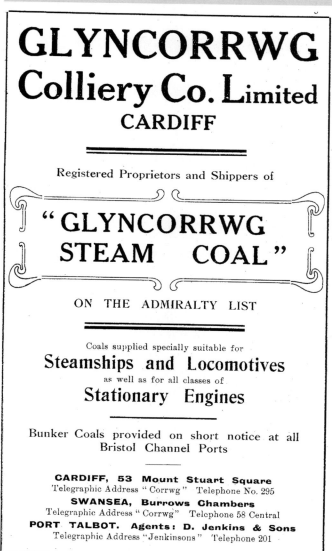

Note: there is no mention in the advertisement of Briton Ferry as on the wagon sides as the registered offices had moved to Cardiff.

The two photographs, taken at the empty and loaded yard at the Clydach Merthyr Colliery in the 1920s, show the company's rolling stock from a variety of manufacturers. The slight differences in the lettering are obvious on close examination, suggesting that the company gave each manufacturer minimal instructions and that the paint shop worked out themselves how the lettering was to be applied. The angles of the photographs do not reveal every wagon number, but at least the difference in appearance, however slight, of wagons built by Wm. Rigley, Charles Roberts and the Gloucester company can be examined. Several wagons are also shown which would appear to be those purchased secondhand or on hire, they are not shown in the surviving Wagon Registers. In the view of the empties the wagons visible are (second row from back): No's 1453, 1684 and 1350; (next row): 1219; (front row): 1444, 1774. The loaded wagons with visible numbers are (front row): 1581, 1413, 8981, 800, 406, 1673; (second row): 532. These photographs emphasise the advice given to modellers when replicating Welsh coal trains, they generally consisted of wagons from a single colliery, there is no visible evidence here of any wagons belonging to coal merchants or factors. However, there will often be variations in livery and visible ownership as mergers and amalgamations throughout the Welsh coalfield were commonplace and the wagon painters were way behind when it came to re-branding, and this should also be borne in mind.

Great Western Collection, NRM

No. 1252 was photographed in November 1906 and was part of an order for 100 wagons numbered 1225-1324 purchased on 10 years deferred payment terms. They were seemingly supplied in two batches, the first 50 (1225-1264) being registered by the Midland Railway, No's 50118-50157. Dimensions are 16ft 0in. x 7ft 4in. x 4ft 0in. and the wagons were painted black with white lettering. This wagon carries the Gloucester owner's number of 43895. The italic lettering on the left reads 'Empty to Clydach Merthyr Colly, Clydach-on-Tawe, Midland Rly.'.

GRC&WCo.

THE GRAIGOLA MERTHYR COLLIERY Co. Ltd

SET amongst a cluster of anthracite producing collieries in the Swansea valley and served by the Midland, LNW and Great Western railways, the Graigola Merthyr Company produced steam coal and between them its two principal collieries wound 550,000 tons a year consistently throughout the inter-war years. Its sales agents were for many years Llewellyn, Merrett & Price, later to become Gueret, Llewellyn & Merrett, and, in turn, a part of Powell Duffryn. Although the Graigola Merthyr company maintained its independence, there were directors common to all companies.

In 1895, the company operated the Birch Rock, Hills Merthyr, Clydach Merthyr and Graigola collieries. By 1913, the modern company was beginning to emerge with some of the older and smaller collieries closed and concentration on Clydach Merthyr at Clydach-on-Tawe, originally owned by the Clydach Merthyr Colliery Co. and later the Graigola Merthyr company, reached by a colliery tramway from a connection on the Midland Railway Swansea Valley line a short distance to the north of Clydach-on-Tawe Station, and the Graig Merthyr Colliery at Pontardulais, which was served by both the LNWR and the Great Western, a drift mine opened by Cory Bros in 1873, redeveloped in 1890 by the West Merthyr Steam Coal Company and to become the Graigola Merthyr Colliery in 1908.

In 1879 a company identified as Compagnie de Houllière de Graigola Merthyr initiated a seemingly endless stream of orders for secondhand wagons and hires of up to 330 wagons at a time from the Gloucester company alone. Accepting that this French owned company was selling the coal to France, the reason for such a huge wagon fleet would be interesting to find out,

particularly as the collieries were only a short distance from the docks at Swansea. The following transactions were recorded:

Compagnie de Houllière de Graigola Merthyr

12.09.1876	55 10-ton, hire 3 years
13.03.1877	115 10-ton, hire 3 months
	100 8-ton, hire 3 months (renewal)
18.09.1878	125 8-ton, 165 10-ton, purchase 7 years
12.03.1879	50 10-ton, weekly hire
14.05.1879	125 8-ton secondhand, hire 3 years
09.07.1879	35 7-ton, hired
14.09.1880	125 8-ton, 165 10-ton secondhand purchased
11.10.1881	114 8-ton, 136 10-ton, hire 3 years
09.01.1883	50 10-ton, hire 1 year secondhand

Graigola Merthyr Co. Ltd

12.01.1886	25 10-ton, hire one month
09.03.1886	316 10-ton, 14 8-ton, hire one year renewal
12.07.1886	25 10-ton, hired one month; 25 10-ton, hired three months
05.04.1887	60 10-ton, hire one year, secondhand, renewal
12.07.1887	20 10-ton, hired one year
12.07.1887	50 10-ton, hire weekly, secondhand
08.11.1887	70 10-ton, hired on daily basis, secondhand, renewal
	46 10-ton, hire weekly, secondhand
	161 10-ton, hire three months, secondhand
10.07.1888	3 8-ton, hire monthly, secondhand
08.08.1888	10 10-ton, hired
13.11.1888	10 10-ton, hire one year, secondhand
	15 10-ton, hire 1 month, secondhand

Photographed in December 1906, No. 1317 is from the second fifty wagons (No's 1265-1342) which were again registered by the Midland (50261-50320). *GRC&WCo.*

11.12.1888	20 10-ton, hire 1 year, secondhand
12.02.1889	25 10-ton, hire 3 months, secondhand
12.03.1889	150 10-ton, hired one year
10.12.1889	150 10-ton, hire one year, secondhand
18.07.1890	3 8-ton, hire 1 year, secondhand
	150 10-ton, hire 2 years, secondhand
	60 10-ton, hire 1 year, secondhand
	23 10-ton, hire 3 months, secondhand
11.11.1894	40 10-ton, hire monthly, secondhand
11.12.1894	40 10-ton, hire one year
10.04.1895	90 10-ton, hire quarterly, secondhand
08.01.1896	50 10-ton, hire monthly, secondhand
11.08.1897	4 7-ton; 6 8-ton; 8 10-ton, hire weekly, secondhand
11.05.1898	4 7-ton; 6 8-ton; 188 10-ton, hire 1 month, secondhand, renewal
14.06.1899	4 7-ton; 6 8-ton; 88 10-ton, hire 1 year, secondhand, renewal
23.05.1900	100 10-ton, purchase 7 years, secondhand
11.06.1900	4 7-ton, 6 8-ton, hire 5 years, secondhand, renewal

For about six years no further transactions were recorded with the Gloucester company, but in 1906 a serious assault was made on the various wagon works with a series of orders which totalled 675 new wagons. Those registered with the Midland Railway are as follows:

20.11.1906	1200 to 1224	Charles Roberts	50093 to 50117
	1225 to 1264	Gloucester	50118 to 50157
	1265 to 1324	Gloucester	50261 to 50320
	1325 to 1374	Wm. Rigley	50208 to 50257
07.02.1907	1375 to 1424	Wm. Rigley	50321 to 50370
21.01.1908	1425 to 1450	Gloucester	55475 to 55500
	1451 to 1624	Gloucester	59001 to 59174
30.08.1909	1675 to 1724	Charles Roberts	63179 to 63228
22.03.1910	1725 to 1774	Charles Roberts	63856 to 63905
29.05.1914	1800 to 1839	S. J. Claye	71961 to 72000
12.06.1915	1840 to 1874	S. J. Claye	74001 to 74035
26.05.1914	1875 to 1949	Harrison & Camm	71861 to 71935

The few missing numbers are assumed to have been registered elsewhere. Also supplied from Gloucester were eleven 'colliers vans', paid for in cash at £135 each.

With a selling agent of the status of Llewellyn, Merrett & Price, who also owned their own wagon fleet, the distribution of the company wagons could have been widespread, the sales agent had offices in both London and Southampton and was well connected with many forms of heavy industry, export and shipping. However, on available evidence it appears that the principal traffic was export.

MODELS : Osborne Models

Of the three hundred wagons supplied to the company by Gloucester RC&WCo, No. 1536 is from the order for two hundred, numbered 1425 to 1624, placed in December 1907 and paid for over ten years. The wagon has seven planks, side and end doors and brakes one side only. Internal measurements are 16ft 0in. x 7ft 4in. x 4ft 2in. Again it is painted black with white letters and carries the same italic 'Empty to' instructions. *GRC&WCo.*

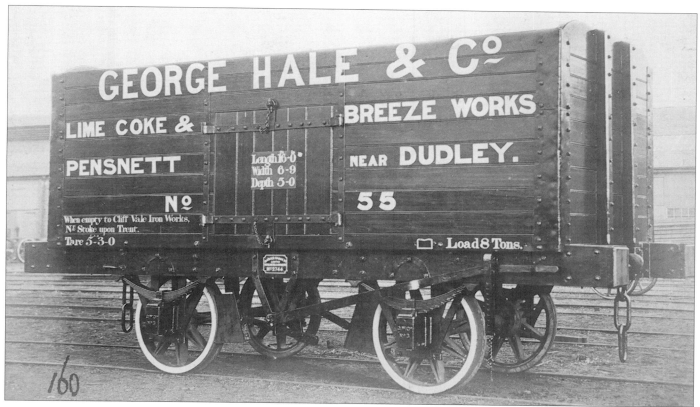

A nine-plank 8-ton wagon with cupboard type doors was supplied by the Gloucester Wagon Co. in November 1871 on five years deferred purchase terms. It carries the rectangular form of the Gloucester builders and owner's plate with the number 2744. Notice the seemingly extended corner plates with a join just above the 5th plank and bolts close together and the cupboard doors. The wagon carries the instructions: 'When empty to Cliff Vale Iron Works, Nr Stoke upon Trent.'.   *GRC&WCo.*

GEO. HALE & Co.

THIS long established company dates back at least to the 1870s, when it was trading at 748 Coventry Road, Birmingham, as builders merchants and breeze suppliers (breeze is coke dust generated during handling). In the 1870s wagons were purchased from the Gloucester Wagon Co. and one of these is shown above. This intriguing nine-plank dumb buffered wagon also shows its owner as having a lime, coke and breeze works (at Pensnett near Dudley) and emptied to the Cliff Vale Iron Works, near Stoke upon Trent. Hale purchased a total of six 8-ton wagons from Gloucester, the first in April 1869, one in each of June, November and December 1871, all on five year terms, and then two for cash in January 1874. A seven year repair contract on all six was signed in March 1879.

The slightly more modern eight-ton seven-plank wagon No. 20, built by Hurst Nelson, extends the business to building material merchants, and whilst its main purpose was to carry coke, it could have been used for several other purposes.

It has been difficult to trace the progression of Hales trading over the years as the company rarely advertised in any local directory: up until 1923 there is little to indicate Hales trading pattern or sources of supply, three that are known are Highley near Kidderminster, Madeley Wood at Wellington and Sneyd at Burslem. It appears that he was more prominent in the Birmingham area than at Stoke-on-Trent during this period of his business.

Hale proclaimed on his wagon sides an association with the Wolstanton Colliery at Etruria, near Stoke-on-Trent, and its Cardox Mined Coals. This shows an affinity with Halls Collieries of Swadlincote, who also boasted a similar process, explained to the author by an old Halls employee as a type of explosive. In fact Cardox used cartridges of liquified carbon dioxide, the expansion of which was gentler than explosives. The Cardox company in its own advertising claimed that it produced much less small coal and dust.

In 1923 Hale ordered two lots of four new wagons from the Gloucester company with his name painted in a most unusual style which may be unique. At the time his advertised address was Birmingham Road, Oldbury, which differs from that painted on the wagons, 20 Cannon Street, Birmingham, an office address listed only intermittently in trade directories, but included in one of 1925. The Oldbury address was the only other known trading location for the next twenty years, with no mention of any business in Stoke-on-Trent apart from the association with the Wolstanton Colliery.

In 1933 four further wagons were hired from Gloucester RC&WCo., followed by a further fifty in October 1936. Another four new wagons were purchased. These differed slightly in appearance from those illustrated (supplied either secondhand or repainted after an overhaul) as the lettering was shaded black.

Wagon No. 20 is of unknown age and dimensions. It is an eight-ton coke wagon with seven planks of varying width, diagonal side braces which do not extend to the top of the wagon, an odd side door arrangement with vertically planked cupboard type doors having a single fastening device and a ring handle, and brakes one side. It was built by Hurst Nelson and is of a type which were reasonably common in the Midlands serving industry with foundry and furnace coke. The wagon appears to be painted dark grey with white letters shaded black and with black ironwork. *courtesy HMRS, ABP726*

Wagon No. 241 is fortunately a lot easier to describe. It is one of four built by the Gloucester RC&WCo. in 1923 and registered with the GWR (Reg. No. 54587). It has seven planks, side and end doors and brakes both sides. The style of lettering, with the principal name in an unusual serif type, is most uncommon and almost distracts from the badly balanced remainder of the livery. It is also unusual for Gloucester wagons which have end doors to be photographed with the end door furthest from the camera, although this might have been done to show off the commode handles! Internally the wagon measured 16ft 0in. x 7ft 5in. x 4ft 3in. and it was painted 'light lead' with white letters shaded black and black vertical ironwork. The wagon number is repeated on the fixed end. The small lettering to bottom right reads 'HEAD OFFICE, GEO. HALE & CO., 20 CANNON STREET, BIRMINGHAM.' and that on underframe '*For repairs advise Wagon Repairs Ltd, Stoke on Trent*'. *GRC&WCo.*

It is apparent from the wagon fleet that the Wolstanton Colliery was the principal source of Hale's business and that Birmingham was most likely as an outlet for its coal. The revitalised colliery in post nationalisation days was one of several selected by the National Coal Board for modernisation. Like many of the others, including such brand new pits at Cotgrave and Bevercotes in Nottinghamshire and Lea Hall at Rugeley, it never fulfilled the promises made of it and closed down in 1985.

The distribution of Hale's wagons would have been limited to the Midlands, Staffordshire, and the parts of Cheshire and Shropshire where Wolstanton coal was sold. It is known that they were seen in Wem in Shropshire. Modellers who have the old Airfix model based on the accompanying illustration should, for accuracy, bear this in mind and remember that it was built in 1924.

MODELS : No. 241, Airfix

Three wagons purchased secondhand or hired from the Gloucester RC&WCo. in the 1930s. All are of seven-plank construction with brakes both sides and side and end doors. Note also the remarkable variation in lettering. Each wagon carries the common features of the italic lettering above the wagon number reading 'Empty to Wolstanton Colliery, Etruria.' and at bottom right 'Head Office, 20 Cannon Street, Birmingham'.

No. 601 appears to have a GWR registration plate dated 1917 with the number 84400. It could have been built originally by the Welsh Wagon Works or Hall, Lewis & Co., both of Cardiff as to the right of the Gloucester hirer's plate is the crown-shaped builder's plate associated with those companies.

No. 604, photographed in February 1933, a month after No. 601, might well date from 1902 but the original registering company cannot be discerned. It is also not of Gloucester origin and carries an oval-shaped builder's plate.

Finally, No. 651, photographed in July 1933. This example is a Gloucester built wagon with the original plate between the legs of the 'V' hanger. All three examples also carry Wagon Repairs Limited plates.

all GRC&WCo.

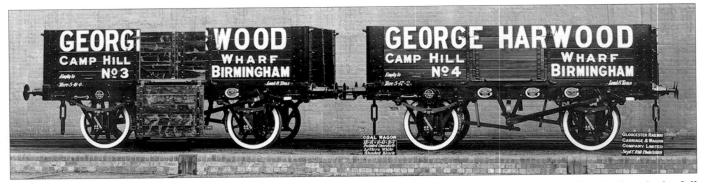

Harwood's wagons No's 3 and 4 were photographed at Gloucester in September 1911. They were of 8-ton capacity with five planks, full height side door and brakes one side only. Dimensions were 15ft 6in. x 6ft 11in. x 3ft 7in. internally. They were painted 'chocolate' with white lettering, shaded black and with black ironwork. *GRC&WCo.*

GEORGE HARWOOD

THIS long standing Birmingham coal merchant was based at the Camp Hill goods station, on the former Midland Railway's original line between Birmingham and Bristol, joining the later line from New Street Station at Kings Norton. Originally working out of an address in Sparkbrook before 1910, Camp Hill was established as a base in the same year and by 1935 an additional depot at Hall Green, GWR, had been added.

The photograph of Camp Hill in *Private Owner Wagons: A First Collection* shows Harwood's wagons dominating, there are at least six in view. Some were purchased new or secondhand from the Gloucester company, and others were hired. Like most coal merchants who still relied on the traditional shovel for unloading, Harwood preferred the smaller eight- and ten-ton wagons, and while Gloucester still had some for hire or sale at reasonable prices, these were obtained in preference to new 12-ton wagons.

Harwood's first known wagons were numbers 3 and 4,

purchased from Gloucester in 1911, followed by numbers 5 and 6, purchased from the Midland RC&WCo. in 1912 (registered Midland Railway 71021 and 71022). Three wagons were purchased from Hunter of Rugby in 1922, numbers 30, 31 and 32. These were registered with the Midland Railway (No's 77950-2) followed by a second order with Gloucester in March 1924, when ten 12-ton wagons, No's 133 to 142 (registered LMS March 24th 1924, No's 74506 to 74515) were purchased and a further ten were hired. A further 22 of the smaller wagons were hired in September 1936 followed by another ten in October 1939.

Harwood patronised several of the Warwickshire and Cannock Chase collieries and those of South Derbyshire. Accordingly his wagons would have been seen in a somewhat limited area. One was photographed empty at Rugby in 1936.

MODELS : None

No. 142 is from a batch of ten wagons delivered in 1924 and registered with the LMS (Reg. No. 94515). It has side doors only, seven planks and brakes on both sides. Internal dimensions were 16ft 1in. x 7ft 7in. x 4ft 4in. and the wheelbase 9ft 0in. As with the wagons above livery was a chocolate body with white letters shaded black and black vertical ironwork. *GRC&WCo.*

The wartime wagon No. 1908 is from a batch of fifteen numbered 1901 to 1915 and was built in 1942 by Charles Roberts & Co. of Wakefield as set out in *Private Owner Wagons: A First Collection*. These 14-ton slope sided steel wagons were a patented design, for which the first large quantities were for Stewarts & Lloyds. It measured 16ft 6in. over headstocks x 8ft 0in. sloping to 6ft 11in. x 4ft 11in. internally. It appears to have a red oxide body with unshaded white lettering. Italic letters at bottom right read: '*Empty to Tunnel Sidings, Stockingford, LMS.*'. The circular plate on the solebar is an owner's plate.   *courtesy HMRS, AAT516*

HAUNCHWOOD COLLIERIES Ltd

THE Haunchwood Colliery Company was formed in 1881 and was the owner of the Haunchwood and Tunnel pits, situated on the Midland Railway line from Nuneaton to Birmingham. The Haunchwood Colliery was about a mile west of the former Midland Railway station at Nuneaton and was closed in 1914 whilst the Tunnel pit, opened in 1894 was almost alongside the Midland's Haunchwood Tunnel three quarters of a mile further west, and was the longer lived of the two.

Haunchwood coal was sent all over the West Midlands and into Northamptonshire, the Thames Valley and London and its surrounding counties. The colliery mined a particularly fine seam of steam coal which was supplied to industrial users, one of the most prominent being the City of Birmingham Gas Department, which purchased Haunchwood steam coal for its locomotives. Haunchwood coal was also supplied for electricity generation at the power stations of the Metropolitan Railway at Neasden, and at Birmingham and Northampton.

Surviving records of the company's wagons are fragmentary, both the Darlington Wagon Co. and Charles Roberts supplied 200 each and smaller quantities were purchased from Midlands builders. In 1906 two hundred wagons were purchased from Thomas Moy of Colchester, registered with the Midland Railway (registration numbers 52479 to 52528 and 52827 to 52976) with side and bottom doors and hinged top planks. These were financed by Sir Alfred Hickman and numbered 1701 to 1900, and judging by the running numbers of the wagons

illustrated no new wagon purchases were made between 1906 and 1942. The wagon fleet was not particularly large, anecdotal unpublished interpretations of the basic livery range from blue to grey, red to brown and black.

The colliery company boardroom was dominated for much of its life until nationalisation by members of the Hickman family of Wolverhampton, headed by Sir Alfred Hickman MP, and on his death in 1910 by three of his sons, themselves heavily involved in the steel industry, owning also for many years the Spring Vale Furnaces of Bilston, later taken over by Stewarts & Lloyds, an association which suggests itself as a major customer for Haunchwood coal.

MODELS : Powsides (transfer)

Three Haunchwood wagons are seen in this cruel enlargement of a postcard view of Weedon. Note, all three show different lettering styles. The middle wagon is numbered 1491.   *John Alsop*

No. 115 of the fleet is from an order for 25 wagons placed with Gloucester RC&WCo. in January 1936 and registered with the LMS (registration number appears to be 157325) and has side and end doors. Empty return instructions are to 'Hendy Merthyr Colliery, Clydach-on-Tawe, Swansea, L.M.S.'. The wagon is painted black with plain white lettering. *GRC&WCo.*

HENDY MERTHYR COLLIERY Co. Ltd
and FELINFRAN COLLIERY Co. Ltd

THE Hendy Merthyr Collieries are by name a misnomer, the term Merthyr was used to describe collieries regardless of whether they were located in the Merthyr area or not, similarly so were such names as Duffryn and Rhondda misused, to promote a type or quality of coal rather than where it came from. This causes some confusion in trying to locate a Welsh colliery titled as such. This practice appears to be peculiar to Wales, as do the addresses on the sides of some Welsh wagons, which invariably show the location of the registered office rather than that of the colliery.

Hendy Merthyr was a latecomer in the field of Welsh coal and mined steam coal in the heart of the anthracite belt near Clydach-on-Tawe, not far from the Graigola Merthyr company's mine, to the north of Swansea on the former Midland Railway Swansea Valley line. The company was registered around 1933 at a time when the Welsh coal trade was in a depressed state, with many mines closing or working on short time, and in addition to developing a new area to the west of Clydach, also revived the name only of the old Felinfran Colliery near Llansamlet, which was working in 1888, ordered twenty new wagons (No's 185 to 204) in 1892 from G. R. Turner of Langley Mill, followed by a further twenty from Whittle of Chorley and closed around 1910. An alternate spelling for this colliery was Velinfran and this may have appeared on the wagon sides. Felinfran also appears as Felin Fran.

The Hendy Merthyr Colliery was a short distance north of Clydach, and looking at a contemporary railway map of the immediate vicinity, its connection with the outside world was buried within the complex of John Player's Clydach Foundry and Tinplate Works. Once clear of this sprawling plant, traffic could proceed via a triangular junction along the former Midland Railway Swansea Valley line towards Swansea, or to the connection with the Neath & Brecon for midlands traffic. Looking at the track layout, it is highly conceivable that some coal produced by this and the Clydach Merthyr Colliery was used at the two Player's plants, to which the track layout is certainly conducive.

Production appears to have commenced in 1935, when 209 miners were employed and an initial order was placed with the Gloucester company for 25 wagons, delivered on October 27th of that year, followed by a further 25 ordered on January 7th of the following year. A little over a year later, a further 100 were ordered from the same source. Fifty of these, as illustrated opposite were lettered and registered for the Felinfran Colliery Co. Ltd, No's 801-850. The wagon builder's records do not show in which livery the remainder were painted. A further 10 13-ton wagons for Felinfran, No's 851-860 were built by Road & Rail Wagons Ltd, Swansea in October 1939.

In 1938 the company was working the Hendy Merthyr pit with 239 personnel, the Tyllwydyn Level being under development with only 29 employees, another new pit at Maesmelyn had not been commenced and the Felin Fran operation was registered as a separate company, with a new Felin Fran Colliery under development with a payroll of 164.

Two wartime wagons built for Hendy Merthyr. Both are of 7-plank construction with side and end doors and disc wheels. No. 1023 was photographed in March 1943 and 1042 in November. Both were painted black with white lettering and the empty instructions imply that the company might actually have seen these wagons.
GRC&WCo.

The Hendy Merthyr company received a further sixty-one 13-ton wagons, No's 1001 to 1061, from Gloucester between March 1943 and November 1946. As part of this wartime order No's 1026-1037 were diverted by Government direction from an order placed by Austin of Cambridge, a company which had shortly before merged with Franklins of Bedford.

By 1945 the Felinfran operation was the largest of the group, the other three could muster only 180 employees and five years later all three had been closed after a lifespan of between ten and fifteen years.

Apart from the possibility of the John Player plant at Clydach, little is known of the market for Hendy Merthyr coal: that new wagons were diverted in wartime conditions in itself suggests that the company had an important government contract,

however, under the circumstances existing at the time they would have been immediately pooled regardless of who the owners were.

No specific advice can be given to the owners of the Dapol model of the Hendy Merthyr wagon (incidentally in the wrong colours) but they would certainly be out of place on any model railway depicting the pre-1936 era, and the Felinfran model would be valid only post 1937. Felinfran is variably spelt as one word or two as 'Felin Fran'. A Hendy Merthyr wagon in the correct colours is available from Osborne Models, as is a Felinfran wagon.

MODELS : Hendy Merthyr, Dapol, Osborne Models
Felinfran: Cambrian, Osborne Models

No. 836 is a similar wagon to No. 115 and from an order for 100 wagons placed in January 1937, the running numbers of which, and the lettering on each wagon, are not known. Empty return instructions are to the Felinfran Colliery, Felinfran, G.W.R. Again, the livery is black with plain white letters. It measures internally 16ft 1in. x 7ft 7in. x 4ft 4in., with a wheelbase of 9ft 0in.
GRC&WCo.

12-ton capacity salt van No. 2300 is from an order for 25 such vehicles produced during wartime by the Gloucester RC&WCo. and although it would not have been pooled, no 'non-pool' identification has been painted on. The small rectangular notice at bottom right reads '*Repairs Advise I.C.I. (Salt) Ltd, Winsford*'. It was registered with the LMS (registration No. 162108) and was painted red with white letters shaded black. The wagon had a length overall of 20ft 6in., whilst length over headstocks was 17ft 6in., height 12ft 0in., width 8ft 0in., and a wheelbase of 10ft 0in. Note that for balance in the lettering layout only two full stops are used in I.C.I.   *GRC&WCo.*

IMPERIAL CHEMICAL INDUSTRIES, SALT DIVISION

THE Salt Division of Imperial Chemical Industries was based in Winsford in Cheshire, along with many other manufacturing activities of this much diversified conglomerate, formed in 1926 by the amalgamation of several makers of dyestuffs, alkalis, chemicals and explosives and substantial involvement in the quarrying of limestone in the Peak District of Derbyshire. Through the absorption of other and smaller companies salt was produced at Stafford and Cheshire, the latter being by far the major source.

The association between ICI (Salt) Ltd and the Gloucester Railway Carriage & Wagon Co. Ltd commenced in 1937, when an order was placed for sixteen open mineral wagons for Stafford. These were numbered 326 to 341 and registered with the LNER (registration numbers 11205 to 11220). In 1942 the company ordered 25 12-ton elliptical roofed salt vans for Winsford, numbered 2300 to 2324 and registered with the LMS (registration numbers 162108 to 162132).

During wartime, production of wagons identified as non-pool and for special purposes continued whenever capacity was available, and further orders were placed with other manufacturers for salt vans for the Winsford and Northwich salt works, and registered with the LMS:

06.06.1940	Northwich	523 to 526	Hurst Nelson
10.04.1942	Winsford	1220 to 1289	Pickering
02.03.1944	Winsford	1290 to 1364	Pickering

These vans were used for the conveyance of salt in bags or in huge blocks, photographs taken inside the Salt Union Works at Bromsgrove show giant slabs being loaded into one of that company's salt vans and others weighing a hundredweight each in drying sheds. Their destinations were invariably chemical works where salt was used extensively, or to food processing plants which relied on large quantities of salt (the fishing industry in particular) as a preservative in the days before commercial refrigeration became a commonplace reality, and as an almost inevitable ingredient in manufactured foods.

MODELS : None

No. 326 was part of the order placed in 1937 for sixteen wagons. It was painted red, lettered white, shaded black and with black ironwork excluding diagonal bracing.   *GRC&WCo.*

LIVERPOOL CORPORATION ELECTRIC SUPPLY

UNLIKE the Liverpool Gas Works, which were privately owned, the Corporation of that city was responsible for its electric supply. The Corporation was an early user of the 20-ton bottom discharge hopper wagon, and between 1924 and 1947 acquired 410, built originally by Cammell Laird at its Nottingham plant and then by its successor, Metro-Cammell at Birmingham. Details of these orders are as follows:

BUILT	No's	BUILDER
1924	1-40	Cammell Laird, Nottingham
09-10.1927	41-80	Cammell Laird, Nottingham
09-10.1929	81-100	Metro-Cammell
03-08.1931	101-140	– ditto –
07-08.1931	141-160	– ditto –
04-05.1935	161-180	– ditto –
09.1936	181-230	– ditto –
01.1937	231-288	– ditto –
01.1938	289-360	– ditto –
1947	361-410	– ditto –

Note: Those wagons supplied in 1947 were actually ordered in 1940.

The wagons themselves were of a considerable size, 21ft 7in. long by 8ft 4in. wide and 7ft 8in. deep, which must have been close to the limits imposed not only by the loading gauge, but would have also prohibited their use at some of the collieries

that the Corporation patronised. The original wagons were lettered with the initials of their owners, later wagons carried the Corporation's full name.

Coal supplies were obtained principally from the Lancashire coalfield and from Scotland (by sea) but towards the end of the 1930s increasing quantities were obtained from Yorkshire and Derbyshire as the following contracts for the year 1937 show:

Stephenson Clarke and Associated Companies Lancashire Associated Collieries Ltd (all in Lancashire)	106,000 tons Bairds and Dalmellingtons (Scotland)
	75,000 tons Hulton
	20,000 tons Haydock
	13,000 tons Sutton Heath
	20,800 tons Wigan Junction
	10,800 tons Park
	20,000 tons Hulton Crompton
	5,000 tons Haydock
	5,200 tons Atherton
John Heaton, Liverpool	10,400 tons Bickershaw (Lancs)
W. Marsh, Liverpool	15,000 tons Wigan (Lancashire)
W. & J. Richardson, Liverpool	15,000 tons Haydock (Lancashire)
Settle Speakman & Co.	80,000 tons Eckington (Derbys)
Daniel K. Rea & Son	15,000 tons Llay Main (N. Wales)
	14,000 tons Brodsworth (Yorks)

Illustrated is wagon No. 31 from the original batch of forty wagons built by Cammell Laird Ltd at their Nottingham plant in 1924 and registered with the LMS (registration numbers 81317 to 81356). It was a 20-ton capacity bottom discharge hopper and was the forerunner of a large fleet which numbered 410 vehicles. The Electricity Department of the Manchester Corporation later bought 100 similar wagons from Metro-Cammell in 1939. The wagon measured 21ft 7in. x 8ft 4in. x 7ft 8in.; wheelbase 12ft 0in. Italic letters at bottom left read *'Return to Liverpool Corporation, Electric Supply Dept, Lister Drive Power Station, Stanley Sidings.'*. Lettering above the handwheel which opens and closes the hopper doors reads on left *'Open'* and on right *'Shut'*. Later wagons in this series had ladders to the side. It is likely that the wagon has been painted for photographic purposes as it is recorded that early wagons were painted black, lettered in plain white L.C.E.S. whilst later examples were 'slate blue' and lettered LIVERPOOL CORPORATION ELECTRICITY DEPARTMENT in 8 inch white letters. These wagons appear to be the only PO wagons built by Cammell Laird. *Birmingham Central Library*

All of the above was slack or very small coal which was ideal for burning in power stations and also had the advantage of being cheaper and more plentiful than other coals. Purchases were also made on the spot market.

The Eckington Colliery was located to the east of Chesterfield and some of the supplies were also obtained from the owners Norwood Colliery nearby, this would most likely have travelled via the Hope Valley route of the LMS. That from Brodsworth near Doncaster on the LNER could have travelled via the Woodhead route, Mottram Yard and the CLC and from Llay Main via Chester and Warrington. Daniel K. Rea & Son were a subsidiary of the Carlton Collieries Association, also owners of the Llay Main Colliery in North Wales. The coal from Bairds & Dalmellingtons was most likely loaded at Glasgow and was discharged at Carriers Dock, Liverpool.

By 1927 most electricity in Liverpool came from the Lister Drive and Clarence Dock generating stations. Lister Drive station, opened in 1900, was served by Stanley Sidings on the LNWRs Bootle Branch. Clarence Dock was a larger station opened in 1931 and its coal was almost exclusively delivered using the 20-ton hoppers. It was reached via Mersey Docks & Harbour Board lines.

With an annual usage of around 430,000 tons, its traffic and wagon movements must have been quite complicated and more than 400 20-ton wagons would have been needed to move it and both colliery and contractors' wagons would also have been needed. In 1938 the Mitchells Main Colliery near Rotherham was an additional supplier but after 1939 supplies reverted to South Lancashire. The hoppers were still used, being marshalled in block trains; their earlier wider wanderings were over.

MODELS : None

D. R. LLEWELLYN & SONS Ltd

DAVID R. Llewellyn commenced a lifetime association with the coal trade in 1906 at the age of 26 with the purchase of the then three year old Windber Colliery near Aberdare, formerly operated by his father Rees Llewellyn, the son of a tenant farmer and formerly surveyor and under manager at the Bwllfa Colliery. Concurrently he purchased ten secondhand wagons from the Gloucester company, from whom he ordered ten new ten-ton wagons in 1907 followed by a further five in the following year. Thirty secondhand wagons were purchased in 1914 followed by fifty new wagons with a simplified livery in the same year.

By 1921, the Llewellyn interests had extended to three more collieries in the Aberdare area, Bwlch, Dyllas and Llwynhellig and other members of the family had been introduced to the business, which traded under the name of D. R. Llewellyn & Sons. The coal marketing firm of Llewellyn Bros of Aberdare and Cardiff were also associated.

From that point on, there was a rapid expansion of the Llewellyn empire and a series of acquisitions, mergers and the reconstitution of several collieries reshaped the entire Welsh coal industry in a few short years. Expansion away from the Aberdare area was achieved by way of acquiring two collieries, Caeglas and Mynydd Sylen, on the Llanelly and Mynydd Mawr Railway to the north of Llanelly in anthracite country, as well as the Tirherbert Colliery at Hirwain, to the west of Aberdare on the Great Western's Vale of Neath line (incidentally the only former Llewellyn colliery still working in 1937). By 1928 Llewellyn had become the chairman of Norths Navigation Collieries Ltd and a director of Guest, Keen & Nettlefold, coal owners and steel producers.

Expansion now proceeded at a breathless pace, and in 1930 the Llewellyn business had been incorporated into Welsh Associated Collieries, a Llewellyn dominated combine into which was merged several large producers of mainly steam coal in the Rhymney, Cynon, Rhondda and Western Valleys. At one swoop such names as Nixons Navigation, Norths Navigation, Hills Plymouth, Cyfartha, David Davis (Ferndale Collieries), Duffryn Rhondda, Bwllfa and Cwmaman and the Cynon Coal Company all lost their individual identities and became part of

Welsh Associated Collieries, as did Guest, Keen & Nettlefold and the colliery agent Gueret Llewellyn & Merrett. All of these companies owned vast fleets of wagons but before the painters could make appreciable inroads into the re-identification programme, Powell Duffryn, which by then had taken a controlling interest in the company, added many more collieries to its portfolio with another round of takeovers. These included Stephenson Clarke and Associated Companies, probably the best known colliery agents and coal factors in the country, whose individual identity was retained, as was Gueret Llewellyn & Merrett, the coal marketing arm of Powell Duffryn and eventual parent company of Stephenson Clarke. It is possible that some of the pre-1927 fleet survived into the war years without being repainted.

The original Llewellyn wagons, meanwhile, may have been seen between collieries and docks and otherwise in the same areas as those of Llewellyn Merrett & Price, with the exception of the Graigola Merthyr collieries but given the rapid expansion of the company and its subsequent ramifications, may have been intermingled with those of its compatriots and travelled just about anywhere before being re-identified.

MODELS : None

An enlargement of the motif as applied to wagons No's 55 and 101 opposite. It is believed to be an impression of a coal cutting machine.

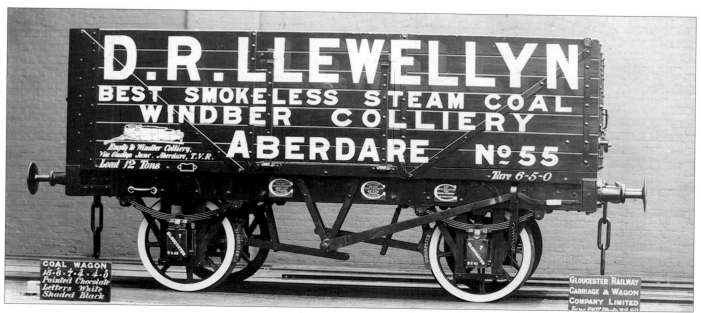

Of the wagons illustrated, No. 55 is from an order for ten 12-ton wagons placed with the Gloucester company in 1907. There may be some reason why the braked side had the end door to the right, on most Gloucester wagons it was to the left as in the case of No. 101 photographed in December 1908. Both were painted chocolate with white letters shaded black. Both are branded '*Empty to Windber Colliery, Via Gadlys Junc. Aberdare, T.V.R.*'. The third wagon, No. 950 from an order for fifty wagons placed in 1914, has a much more simplified livery of black with plain white lettering. It is a 12-ton wagon with side and end doors, seven planks and brakes on both sides. Measurements are (internally) 16ft 0in. x 7ft 4in. x 4ft 2in. Italic letters at bottom left read: '*Empty to Dyllas Colliery, G.W.R. Aberdare*'.   all GRC&WCo.

It is not possible to determine the size of the order placed with the Gloucester company from which wagon No. A4520 was delivered, as the records for this period are missing. However, it is possible that it is from an order placed by H. G. Lewis for 200 wagons, the end user of some 90 of these vehicles has never been discovered. At the time of delivery, in March 1923, the company was a thriving and fast expanding trader in Welsh coal, as well as the owner of an equally vibrant shipping company. The connection with Southampton may have been a purely maritime one, no office was recorded at that seaport, which was the second largest in the country in terms of inbound coal tonnage, but also received a lot of Welsh coal by rail as several large local merchants directed their wagons accordingly. The wagon measured (I.D.) 16ft 0in. x 7ft 4in. x 4ft 2in. Painted black with white letters and the italic lettering at bottom left reads *'Empty to Graig Merthyr Colliery, Pontlliw, G.W.R.'*. The Graig Merthyr Colliery is decribed in more detail in this volume under its owners, the Graigola Merthyr Colliery Co. The italic script on the solebar reads *'Repairs advise C. S. Arthur Ld, 32, Park Place, Cardiff.'*. GRC&WCo.

D. R. LLEWELLYN, MERRETT & PRICE (LONDON) Ltd

THE photograph of this wagon may suggest on the surface to represent a coal merchant or exporter based in London and Southampton, but in actual fact it represents a small part of the career of Sir David Richard Llewellyn, the most prominent figure in the south Wales coal industry.

Llewellyn Merrett & Price was also engulfed in the rapid consolidation of the ownership of the south Wales collieries and following a merger with rival L. Gueret & Sons, shipowners, patent fuel manufacturers, coal factors and exporters, became Gueret, Llewellyn & Merrett. There were then four members of the Llewellyn family on the board of directors as well as H. H. Merrett, a name which will also become familiar in the Welsh coal trade. Roger W. Price, seemingly almost superfluous in such exalted company, was a director of this and other companies such as Merrett Bros, ship brokers, insurance brokers and chartering agents, as well as managers of a fleet of steamships, presumably colliers, owned by Llewellyn, Merrett & Price Limited. That the company was also located in Southampton as well as the principal South Wales ports is an indication that its wagons travelled to that port as well as London. The company was also represented overseas with offices in Paris and New York. Agencies were held for other Welsh colliery companies which at the time were independent of the emerging empire that Llewellyn was in the process of building.

In 1930 most of the Llewellyn owned companies were dissolved and a new company, Welsh Associated Collieries was formed with Gueret, Llewellyn & Merrett as sales agents. Much of this may be considered peripheral to the subject of Private Owner Wagons, but it is in fact central to the subject as a sequence of owners also represents a series of changes of livery and identification.

It is also unnecessary to point out that these organisations combined owned what must have been a fifth of the estimated 125,000 Private Owner wagons in use in Wales by the time this chain of amalgamations had been completed. In the instance of wagons from south Wales, which were invariably registered with the Great Western Railway, that very few of that company's records have survived makes tracing their progression and re-identification virtually impossible.

With the ramifications of the organisation, Llewellyn Merrett & Price wagons could have been seen almost anywhere, as were those of its successors, and as a lot of Welsh coal was sent to Southampton for local use and bunkering, this would justify the lettering on the wagon illustrated. Conversely, as it emptied to the Graig Merthyr Colliery of the Graigola Merthyr company it could have been used in nothing more than a humdrum shuttle between the colliery and the Swansea Docks.

MODELS : None

LONDON BRICK Co. & FORDERS Ltd

THE towering chimneys of brickworks rose from the basically flat landscape around Peterborough and Bedford, where the biggest brick producers in the country located their works. The London Brick Company had substantial operations at Fletton, near Peterborough; the Northam works at Eye, Peterborough; nearby Dogsthorpe and Whittlesey and at Millbrook, on the former LNWR line from Bletchley to Bedford. Forders had works at Bedford; Harlington, Bedfordshire; Bulkington, (LNWR) near Nuneaton; and Millbrook (LNWR), Bedfordshire. The company also owned the Marston Hall Quarries (LNWR) near Nuneaton, the Sewell Lime Works at Stanbridgeford (LNWR); and had a brick siding at Dove Holes (LNWR). The two companies amalgamated in 1923 and subsequently expanded by means of further acquisitions.

Early in 1932 the company ordered 25 20-ton steel hopper wagons numbered 1001 to 1025 from the Birmingham Railway Carriage and Wagon Company, a single wagon being delivered to the Griff Colliery at Nuneaton and the rest delivered empty to the Shipley Colliery near Ilkeston. The came a sequence of small orders with Charles Roberts delivered between June 1933 and March 1936 totalling 37 wagons, which were very similar to those that were built for Stephenson Clarke. Based on the photograph of No. 1029, the famous hod carrier 'Fred' was left off of these wagons, yet was restored in 1937 when after a change of name, the entire fleet was to have been re-identified.

The new livery was a black body, 'London Brick Company Limited' in seven-inch red letters on the second plank down, 'Phorpres' Bricks' in ten inch letters occupying centrally the third and fourth planks in white letters, the hod carrier on the bottom three planks of the wagon door in black on a red pentagon, a white panel on the bottom plank at bottom left with the wagon number, and the company address on the third plank at the left. The same livery layout was to be used for the steel hoppers.

The source of coal for the various brickworks would have been collieries in Notts and Derbyshire, Warwickshire and South Leicestershire, travelling to the brickworks via the Great Northern, Midland and LNWR main lines. However, it is considered that the large hoppers worked principally to the Shipley Colliery, known to have facilities to handle such large vehicles.

Veteran Hornby Dublo modellers will remember the tinplate reproductions of the bogie LNER braked bogie open forty-ton brick wagon. Modellers today have the choice of a Bachmann 12-ton open wagon and a Powsides transfer. These are both based on an interim livery which most likely existed between 1923 and 1937, although some may not have received the new livery before they were pooled.

> MODELS : None (both Bachmann and Powsides produced a 12-ton seven plank wagon)

'Take out locking pin and pull over handle as far as possible before turning wheel to open door. After closing door, push back handle and replace locking pin.'. So goes the instructions on the large hopper wagons built for Stephenson Clarke by Charles Roberts, of similar design and capacity to that illustrated. And so are repeated these instructions to the London Brick men whose responsibility it was to oversee their unloading. The identification of the wheel on the wagon side as 'Wheel for hopper door' was common to both owners. The dimensions of these wagons are unknown, but overall they must have been at the limits of the loading gauge and are probably the same as those of the Liverpool Corporation. Painted black with white letters, which appear to be shaded in a very pale colour, possibly cream. There is also very small lettering around the rim of the hopper door wheel which reads 'OPEN → THIS IS NOT A BRAKE ← SHUT'.

courtesy HMRS, AAS120

LONDONDERRY COLLIERIES Ltd

ONE of the largest suppliers of coal to the London market was the Londonderry Colliery company, whose pits were located in the Seaham area of Durham, and who operated their own private railway from the coalfields to Seaham Harbour, from where most of their coal was shipped. Like many of the colliery companies in the Durham/Northumberland coalfield, the company owned their own fleet of 20-ton wooden bodied hopper wagons specifically for traffic between the pits and the coal loading points and were not regularly used for traffic elsewhere. This was the precedent of the North Eastern Railway and was a welcome advancement on the laborious methods of transporting coal elsewhere in the country. Unfortunately, although there were other instances of constant short-haul traffic in large quantities on a regular basis in other parts of the country, there was little enthusiasm or incentive to follow the North Eastern's lead.

The principal collieries of the Marquis of Londonderry were the Dawdon, Seaham and Vane Tempest at Seaham Harbour, which between them produced annually 1,600,000 tons of household, gas, steam and manufacturing coal which was not only sold locally for all of those purposes, but shipped by coastal collier, principally to gas works and power stations. Coal was also shipped to Southampton, Portsmouth, Ipswich, Colchester, Bristol and Poole, and probably elsewhere around the British coast. The gas works at Aldershot also used Londonderry coal almost exclusively, this being shipped, apparently to Rochester,

the third largest port in the country for the landing of domestic coal (1912 figures) and then transferred to railway wagons, as there were such facilities at some of the coal docks. Much of this traffic was sold direct to the end consumer, such large concerns as the Gas Light and Coke Company and the South Metropolitan Gas Co. of London owned their own fleet of colliers, as did the giant coal factors Stephenson Clarke and Wm Cory.

It was to the numerous gas works and power stations in London that the heaviest traffic for Tyneside coal was despatched. The Gas Light and Coke Company contracted for 350,000 tons of Londonderry coal in six months in 1919, among other large users were the Commercial Gas Company and the South Suburban Gas Company.

The wagon illustrated was limited to local use between the collieries and the staithes at Seaham and Sunderland harbours, and was probably exempted from pooling, as it was designed for a specific purpose and ran mainly on private lines. Its delivery run from works to owner would have been under the 'one journey only at reduced speed' carded principle. Its inclusion was warranted as very few illustrations of wagons of this type have appeared in a publication such as this.

MODELS : None

The wagon illustrated was built in 1934 by Charles Roberts as one of an order for 100 numbered from 101 to 200. Application was made to the LNER for registration but this was declined under the basis 'to run only on the owners own lines'. This wagon is typical of those which had been used for many decades in the Durham coalfield. A similar batch was built by Charles Roberts for the Londonderry Colliery in 1922. These hopper wagons had fixed ends and were discharged at staithes. Note the shunters steps and grabrails for use by the men working on the inclines, which might also explain the outsize handbrake lever which would enable a man on the step to operate it. The wagon measured (I.D.) 19ft 7in. x 7ft 7in. (at top) x 6ft 10in. deep. It appears to be painted grey with plain white letters. Small lettering at bottom right reads 'TO RUN BETWEEN DAWDON COLLIERY, SEAHAM AND SUNDERLAND DOCKS ONLY.'. Between Dawdon Colliery and Seaham Harbour they would have run on private lines but a trip to Sunderland would involve travelling over the main line. *courtesy HMRS, AAS327*

Built by R. Y. Pickering of Wishaw, No. 511 is a seven-plank 12-ton wagon with side and end doors and was delivered in 1903 and registered with the Great Northern Railway. Its livery appears to be a red body with black ironwork and white letters shaded black.

courtesy HMRS, ACH225

LOW LAITHES COAL Co.

THE company operated two collieries, Low Laithes, located on a short mineral branch near Flushdyke on the former Great Northern Railway Wakefield to Dewsbury line, usually known as the Ossett Branch, and Wrenthorpe, a short distance (about a half-mile) north of Wakefield Westgate Station on the eastern side of the Great Northern Leeds main line. The Low Laithes Colliery was in production in 1895 but probably dates back considerably earlier, as it was in decline in 1923 when its personnel had been reduced to a little over 200, and the Wrenthorpe pit was providing the bulk of production, with a personnel of over 1,700. The company did not at any time provide statistics which would indicate how much coal was raised, but in comparison with the known production at Nostell which was only a short distance from Wakefield it is suggested that between the two pits 5,000 tons a week would be a reasonable figure.

The collieries produced manufacturing, household and gas coal, and whilst the first two would have found their main markets in the South Yorkshire area, Low Laithes gas coal reached a much wider market. The company was a long time supplier to the City of Birmingham with up to 50,000 tons per year, 1,000 tons a week or between 100 and 120 wagon loads, a major supplier to the gas works at Coventry, Bradford, Leeds and Manchester, and outside of the general area to gas works at Lincoln and Whitby. Exports via Hull alone were 127,754 tons in 1913.

During the first world war the company had a substantial contract with the Gas Light and Coke Company, whose supplies were normally received by sea from the Newcastle area at its various riverside gas works upstream from London on the River Thames. In 1919 the Thames Coal Company of London was awarded a contract for 21,000 tons of Low Laithes coal, the transportation of which would have at that time been via the Great Northern main line.

On January 3rd, 1928, receivers and managers were appointed to the company. A minute in the records of the Lincoln Corporation Gas Works reported that the collieries had closed and no further supplies could be expected, but it is known that the company was not in liquidation. There is no explanation for this sudden closure, the Low Laithes Colliery was obviously close to being worked out, but Wrenthorpe appears to have been still viable as the company was accepting new contracts for gas coal up to six months before its closure.

The distribution of Low Laithes wagons would have been mainly in the Yorkshire area, but also to Coventry, Birmingham, Lincoln and Manchester. London traffic may have been restricted to wartime via the Great Northern main line. For modellers, these wagons would have to be restricted to layouts depicting periods before 1930. After the collieries closed, some were known to have been working from the Briggs collieries near Normanton.

MODELS : None

Twenty five new wagons at £69 each were ordered in December 1899 from Gloucester and delivered in the following year. No. 568 has seven planks, side and end doors, inside diagonal bracing and brakes one side only. It measured 14ft 5in. x 6ft 11in. x 4ft 0in. and was painted black with white letters. Italic letters at bottom left read 'For Repairs advise North Central Wagon C° L^d, Swansea.'. Note also the unusual position of the tare weight.   GRC&WCo.

MAIN COLLIERY Co. Ltd

COAL was mined in the district surrounding Neath Abbey as early as 1806, and by 1869 the Neath Abbey Coal Co. was formed by the Neath Abbey Ironworks and over the succeeding thirty years the company's trading name was changed frequently. In 1880 it became the Duffryn Main and Neath Abbey United Coal Co. and in 1892 the Dynevor Duffryn Colliery Co., which sank the Duffryn Main pit at Skewen, to the west of Neath, in that year. This was not far from Neath Abbey which was the centre of the company's operations which consisted of the Brithdir, Court Herbert, Tir Edmund, Duffryn Main, Bryndewy, Waurnfirch and New Winning collieries.

The Main Colliery Co. Ltd was formed in June 1889 with Duffryn Main as its principal pit and five others, extending from Neath to Skewen and Llansamlet on the Great Western main line between Neath and Swansea. A 1905 photograph shows Duffryn Main Colliery with a line of Main wagons, numbers above the wagon door, included.

Coal from the Dynevor Duffryn Colliery was supplied for many years to the Corporation of the City of London for various pumping stations and other works where high quality steam coal was required. This was sold through the London coal factor Dinham Fawcus & Co. Ltd. Unfortunately Dynevor Duffryn coal declined in quality during the early part of the twentieth century, and Dinham Fawcus were obliged to redirect their business to the collieries of the Ocean company in the Rhondda Valley.

Main's collieries declined during the 1920s and were successively closed until by 1929 all had ceased production. One unidentified colliery remained open in 1945 with a personnel of seven, as a maintenance or pumping station. There was an indirect association with the Neath Abbey Patent Fuel Company (see page 88).

The company obviously took over a fleet of wagons as in April 1890 a repair contract was taken with the GRC&WCo. on 94 10-ton wagons. In May the company hired seventy 10-ton wagons from Gloucester for one year and placed orders for new wagons in 1895 (25) and 1899 (25). In both instances they were paid for in cash.

Wagons owned by the Main Colliery would have been seen mainly locally and between South Wales and London. There is no evidence of anything but a small fleet and the solitary model would be out of place on any model railway layout based on a period of after the early 1930s.

MODELS : Powsides

Left: The Main Colliery features on the left of this postcard view of Drymma Head.   *Pope/Parkhouse Archive*

86

No. 8, photographed in September 1898, is a six-plank wagon with side doors only, brakes one side and internal diagonal bracing. It was purchased secondhand on deferred purchase terms having first been registered with the LNWR in 1891 (No. 109) and carrying the Gloucester owner's number of 28912. In this it is unusual in that Gloucester have put a full description board in front of the wagon. It measured (I.D.) 14ft 5in. x 6ft 11in. x 3ft 8in. and was painted 'lead colour' with white letters shaded black and black ironwork.

GRC&WCo.

MORRIS & HOLLOWAY

MORRIS & Holloway, with an office at 31 Commercial Road and a coal depot at Barrs Court Station, on the Great Western Railway but into which the London & North Western had access from its south Wales lines and the Midland from Brecon via Hay-on-Wye and by running rights over the Great Western from Worcester, thus had access to the steam coal producing mines of the Sirhowey and Western Valleys, the anthracite producing pits of the Swansea Valley, and the coalfields of the Midlands. They were also, according to their early wagons, both lime and salt merchants.

The company dealt regularly with Evans Reid & Co. of Cardiff, sales agents for the Partridge Jones collieries to the north of Newport, travelling direct via Abergavenny. An example being a single order placed in 1938 for 1,000 tons Ebbw Vale peas (small graded coal often known as pea slack) for the Hereford Hospital, foundry coke, coal for the Hereford and

Tredegar Brewing Co. and for general sale from the ex-John Lancaster collieries. Coal was also obtained from the Cannock Chase and Warwickshire coalfields.

The company placed its first order for new wagons with the Gloucester company in 1898 and further orders were placed in 1911. Subsequently there are no recorded new wagon purchases but this is not important as coal merchants such as Morris & Holloway frequently obtained them on the secondhand market.

The range of these wagons would have been from Hereford to South Wales via the Great Western/LNWR route and to the collieries of Cannock Chase and Warwickshire. They could have also been seen delivering coal to the smaller wayside stations within Herefordshire and along the Welsh border.

MODELS : Slaters

The line-up of four wagons numbered 4, 5, 6 and 7 was captured on film in July 1911. All had the foldover top door above the wagon side door and are shown with the various door arrangements. They have side doors only and internal diagonal bracing and measured 14ft 6in. x 6ft 11in. x 4ft 0in. Unlike No. 8 these are painted dark red with white letters shaded black and black ironwork.

GRC&WCo.

NEATH ABBEY PATENT FUEL Co. Ltd

PATENT Fuel comes in the form of manufactured solid fuel in block form and is made from coal dust or unsaleable coal rubble to which is added an inflammable, binding and adhesive component (pitch), which is then formed under a pressure of approximately two tons per square foot into a moulded and uniform shape.

In this instance the Neath Abbey Patent Fuel Co. Ltd described their product as anthracite ovoids, the shape and size of which varied from a large hens egg to that of an ostrich or larger. That they were made from anthracite, the King of coals and the most expensive to both mine and purchase, indicates that the company in all probability purchased otherwise unsaleable leftovers from the many anthracite mines in the vicinity of its plant at Garnant, on the Great Western branch from Pantyffynnon to Brynamman, and a further works at Jersey Marine, on the Rhondda and Swansea Bay Railway.

Little information can be found about the company, except that its short history must have been quite a turbulent one. It has been included as it shows considerable insight into the movement of wagons which have been resold and the subsequent wide geographical range in which they spent their working lives.

On March 22nd, 1923 an order was placed with the Gloucester company for 100 12-ton wagons on the basis of a long term hire with the option of purchase. These were delivered in May of that year and presumably numbered 1 to 100.

It was obvious in the following year that the quarterly payments could not be maintained, and the company was in financial trouble. By March 1927 payments were 21 months behind and Gloucester was owed £4,520 10s. in overdue instalments. The financial position of Neath Abbey Patent Fuels was soon found to be a precarious one. In 1929 the Gloucester company accepted an agreement in which £3,000 was repaid in three instalments over six months, but recording in the minutes that any pressure for more immediate repayment would send the company into bankruptcy.

It is obvious that the wagons were repossessed by April of 1928 as the Gloucester company began selling them off and the following individual sales were recorded:

6 to Cheltenham Gas Works	£90 each cash
10 to Nottingham Corporation Gas Works	£93 each cash
20 to A. R. Banks, West Blaina Colliery	
2 to C. & E. Collieries, Glyn Neath	£102 each cash
2 to Robert Vasey	
2 to Gas Light & Coke Co.	
20 to Chemical & Metallurgical Industries, Runcorn	
7 to Cheltenham Gas Works	£100 each cash
3 to D. Isaac and Co.	
2 to J. Collier, Neath	

Where no cash amount is shown wagons were purchased on deferred payment terms or hired out. This accounts for 74 of the 100 wagons, the others were probably hired out immediately.

MODELS : None

From the order placed in 1923 with the Gloucester company for 100 7-plank wagons with side and end doors and brakes both sides. It saw very little service under this owner and was returned to the builder and subsequently resold. Measuring (I.D.) 16ft 0in. x 7ft 4in. x 4ft 2in. it was painted black with white letters. Italics at bottom left read '*Empty to Neath Abbey Patent Fuel Works, Jersey Marine, R. & S. B. Rly Section, G.W.R.*'.

GRC&WCo.

Photographed in 1949 with most of its pre-war lettering intact and no indication of utility lettering, No. 375 is one of two hundred wagons purchased second hand in 1929 from Stanley Bell (Wagons) Ltd of Stockport. It has side, end and bottom doors and was originally registered with the Great Northern Railway. Although it bears a builders plate it is unreadable, but the possibility of it being built by Stablefords of Coalville should be considered, as many wagons in which Bell traded on the second hand market came from that builder. The wagon was painted black with plain white letters. Note that the letter 'S' in 'NOSTELL' has a pronounced lean, while the 'T' is completely out of alignment, and no address or empty return instructions remain on the wagon. The solebar bears a paint date which is also indistinct. In other words a 'colliery workshop' repaint carried out with maximum economy. *courtesy HMRS, AAK127*

NOSTELL COLLIERY

THE colliery was located about ten miles to the south-east of Wakefield alongside the former Great Northern Railway Doncaster to Leeds main line. It produced gas, steam and household coal which was distributed mainly in the West Riding of Yorkshire and in Lancashire. By Yorkshire standards it was a small operation, producing only 165,000 tons a year in the 1920s, some 350 to 400 wagon loads weekly. In common with many small to medium sized collieries in Yorkshire, the company owned a modest fleet of about 400 wagons, many of those recorded on its roster during the mid-1920s being of eight- and ten-ton capacity and built by Charles Roberts of Wakefield in 1888 and 1891. The ownership of the fleet was mixed, about half were owned by the company and the rest on long term hire.

The colliery transacted a lot of its business through Stanley Bell (Wagons) Limited, of Reddish, near Stockport and also hired wagons through the North Central Wagon Company of Rotherham. In 1928 the company had on hire 200 10-ton wagons rebuilt by Stanley Bell and numbered 1 to 200; a further fifty on hire from the North Central Wagon Company and given scattered numbers between 401 and 470 plus No. 515. These were of 12-ton capacity and built by Stableford of Coalville.

An offer was made by Stanley Bell on June 25th 1928 for 70 wagons built in 1924 by Stableford for Fox of Derby. These were of twelve-ton capacity with side, end and bottom doors. Several were standing at that time at Barrow Main Colliery near Barnsley for inspection. This does not appear to have been taken up.

On May 6th, 1929, the company purchased, also from Stanley Bell, 200 rebuilt ten-ton wagons for £90 each, these were numbered from 201 to 400. A surviving LNER Wagon Rebuild Register shows that they were re-registered in October 1930, the original registration numbers with the Great Northern Railway were scattered between 490 and 1414. As the Great Northern registration books are no longer with us, it has been impossible to trace who the original owners were, but the registration numbers suggest building dates in the 1890s. A trade-in of £25 each was allowed for 178 of the old Roberts wagons, which had seen many years service, some since 1888.

Further orders were placed with this builder in December 1928 for 100 wagons, and a further 100 in April 1929. Against the second order 100 old wagons were to be traded in, but 25 of these were retained for internal use at the colliery. Stanley Bell (Wagons) Ltd were taken over shortly afterwards by the Derbyshire Railway Carriage and Wagon Company, it is not known if the transaction was completed.

Consumers of Nostell coal who have been recorded were the Bradford Borough Council Gas Department for up to 9,000 tons a year during the years 1914 to 1918, for which records have survived, and the Wakefield Gas Company for 2,500 tons per annum during the 1920s. This is not a true indication of the colliery's trading, for there are very few records of consumers of any category remaining from this area.

MODELS : None

NOTTINGHAM CORPORATION GAS DEPARTMENT

IT was in 1819 that the Nottingham Gas Light & Coke Company commenced producing town gas at Eastcroft, a site not far from the centre of Nottingham, and, like many early gas works, close to the canal network. In 1874, the enterprise was taken over by the Corporation of Nottingham. The original plant was by then also served by the Great Northern Railway, whose London Road passenger station was almost adjacent. Further railway development saw the gas works surrounded by the London & North Western goods sheds and the Midland Railway, which also had access. Already denied expansion, the site became even more cramped when the Great Northern was extended on a viaduct, which cut through the gas works, to its new London Road Station and the connection at Weekday Cross Junction with the new London Extension main line of the Great Central and Nottingham Victoria Station. Remarkably, the gas works outlasted the railway and was not closed until 1970, when the production of coal gas in Nottingham ceased.

Two other gas works, Radford (1844) and Basford (1854), were located on the western fringe of Nottingham, alongside the former Midland Railway Leen Valley line between Nottingham and Basford stations. Radford was on the eastern side of the railway and although it possessed a private siding, did not use locomotives within the gas works. The works were closed in 1940 and the site sold to a venerable Nottingham institution, the Raleigh Cycle Company. The Basford Gas Works were by far the largest, occupying a substantial area on the west side of the railway, the site being still evident today where the Nottingham Ring Road crosses the Leen Valley railway and effectively splits it.

The Gas Department also owned a chemical plant at Giltbrook, near Kimberley and connected to the former Midland Railway mineral branch from Bennerley Junction, on the Erewash Valley line to the Digby and New London collieries. The siding serving the works was recorded as the Nottingham Corporation Chemical Works Siding. The Digby Colliery was closed in 1937 when its owners merged with the Bestwood and Babbington Colliery companies, who had previously merged in 1936 to form B. A. Collieries Limited (see *Private Owner Wagons: A First Collection*) but the sidings which served them were left for a further four years until the chemical works were closed and dismantled. Shunting the chemical works was carried out by a colliery locomotive.

Wagons known to have been owned by the Gas Department are listed below, and have been taken from the Midland and LMS wagon registers and the company minutes.

1892	303	Roberts	tank wagon (?)
1898	149 to 158	Metropolitan	10-ton open
1906	80 to 87	Claye	10-ton open
1906	76, 77, 78, 79	Claye	tank wagons, Midland 51914-51917
1906	169	Metropolitan	hopper (steel), Midland 42188
	3 wagons		open, s/hand from J. Beadman
1912	6 wagons		open 12-ton, s/hand from J. C. Abbott
1914	82, 83, 306, 307	Claye	Sulphate of ammonia tank wagons
1915	6 wagons	F. Wright, Bagthorpe	10-ton open, new
1915	10 wagons	F. Wright, Bagthorpe	open, s/hand

1915	1 wagon	Midland	acid tank wagon, cost £190
1916	9 wagons	F. Wright, Bagthorpe	open, s/hand
1917	26 wagons	Longstaff, Hednesford	open, 8-ton s/hand
1917	4 wagons	Longstaff, Hednesford	open, 10-ton secondhand
1922	5 wagons	H.M. Disposals	oil tank wagons, 10-ton, cost £240 each
	2 wagons	H.M. Disposals	acid tank wagons, 12-ton, cost £200 each.
1923	351-405	Wm Rigley	12-ton open, LMS 83768-83822
1925	124, 158, 335, 379, 476	H.M. Disposals	tank wagons, cost £225 each
1926	508, 509	S. J. Claye	tank wagons, LMS 101739-40
1928	10 wagons	Gloucester	12-ton open, s/hand, cost £93 each
1929	528	Midland	welded tank wagon, LMS 106483
1939	416-435	Wm Rigley	12-ton open, LMS 166526-166545

Whereas the minutes of the Department are very detailed in many respects of its day to day operation, they are, like many other wagon owners, quite vague when referring to their wagon fleet. There are, for example, no references to tank wagon No. 69, purchased from G. R. Turner of Langley Mill, or of tank wagon No. 74, built by Hurst Nelson, of which there are photographs in existence. Rigley's twenty new 12-ton wagons supplied in 1939 were not delivered until October of that year, referred to as 20-ton wagons but the Wagon Register interpretation of their load capacity is preferred. They would have almost certainly been immediately pooled. The ten wagons purchased secondhand from the Gloucester Railway Carriage and Wagon Company are recorded as being originally owned by the Neath Abbey Patent Fuel Works (see page 88) and may have been numbered 406 to 415.

Gas coal for the three works was sourced from traditional areas, and contracts are recorded in the departmental minutes in varying detail. The Gas Department was also responsible for the purchase of coal for both the City Engineers and Education Departments of the City of Nottingham, therefore recorded contracts include supplies from collieries which are not known to have produced gas coal (e.g. Annesley) and such coal could have been distributed all over the city as well as the City Engineers Department depot at Eastcroft, on the opposite side of the Midland Railway to the gas works.

What is notable is the large amount of cannel coal used. The corporation purchased it regularly up until the 1920s from the Clifton Colliery, on the banks of the River Trent on the immediate outskirts of the city, and the Babbington Colliery, on the A610 where the present Park-and-Ride facility stands today. What is intriguing about these two contracts is that Clifton was instructed at one time to deliver their cannel 'by cart to Eastcroft works', obviously making the mile journey in one ton lots several times a day at a leisurely pace. Equally intriguing are the supplies of cannel from the Babbington Colliery to the Basford Gas Works, the distance involved was less than a mile and must rank as the shortest journey covered by a railway wagon, but the annual supplies were as much as 33,000 tons or seventy wagon loads a week. It was also purchased from the Swanwick Colliery near Ripley. Cannel was an additive to normal gas coal to produce a brighter light, and was often produced by collieries which did not normally produce gas coal themselves.

Regular contractors for the supply of gas coal read like a roster of the most noted names in the trade with two strange exclusions, the Birmingham firms of Wilson, Carter and Pearson Ltd, and Evesons (Coals) Ltd. Contracts were let in May, 1933 as follows:

CONTRACTOR	TONNAGE	ORIGIN
J. C. Abbott & Co. Ltd, Birmingham	10,000 tons	Clay Cross (Derbys.)
	15,000 tons	Waleswood (Yorks.)
	10,000 tons	Tibshelf (Derbys.)
Jonathan Longbotham & Sons, Sheffield	14,000 tons	Sutton (Notts.)
	15,000 tons	Ireland, Markham Main (Derbys.)
	17,000 tons	Shipley (Derbys.)
	5,000 tons	Renishaw Park (Derbys.)
	10,000 tons	Tinsley Park (Yorks.)
T. Cash & Co., Birmingham	20,000 tons	Swanwick (Derbys.)
J. & G. Wells, Chesterfield	10,000 tons	Holbrook (Derbys.)
Butterley Co., Codnor Park	15,000 tons	Ormonde (Derbys.)
E. Wild, Kimberley	7,500 tons	Pilsley (Derbys.)
W. N. Toft, Derby	10,000 tons	Riddings (Notts.)
Stephenson Clarke, London	5,000 tons	Glapwell (Derbys.)
Hardwick Colliery, Heath, Chesterfield	20,000 tons	Hardwick (Derbys.)
Cawood Wharton & Co., Leeds	7,000 tons	Renishaw Park (Derbys.)

(This latter contract was placed six months later and replaced a previous contract which was seriously behind in deliveries.)

These contracts were let unusually on a 'call in as required' basis, which to say the least is unusual for a large user. This procedure was not repeated, as the Corporation awarded contracts for 156,000 tons of coal in October of the following year, suggesting that the 190,500 tons contracted for in May 1933 lasted for eighteen months.

Of the above collieries, Shipley was never noted as a gas coal producer although for a time the Kilburn seam that it worked produced small quantities, for which the Nottingham Corporation appears to be the sole customer. However, the colliery did produce excellent manufacturing and household fuels. Notably, all of the above collieries were on the former Midland Railway lines of the LMS, who enjoyed almost a monopoly of the gas works traffic, even though in 1934 the LNER laid sufficient siding space at the Eastcroft Works to hold a further fifty wagons. All of the coal used at Giltbrook was supplied by the adjacent Digby Colliery until it was closed shortly before the chemical plant was also out of use.

There were also many purchases on the spot market, collieries participating in 1924 (when all of these transactions were reported in full) were Annesley, Sherwood, Babbington and Shipley for household or industrial coal, and Glasshoughton, Staveley, Old Silkstone, Unstone, Glapwell, Pilsley, Nunnery and Shipley for gas coal. An order for 100 wagons of Annesley coal was specified to be sent by the LNER to the Eastcroft Works depot. Additional coal factors who benefited from this business were Spencer Abbott and Co. and Evesons of Birmingham,

Identical to several hundred such vehicles built for the City of Birmingham Gas Department (see *Private Owner Wagons: A First Collection*) No. 169 was a solitary example produced for the Nottingham Gas Works, who, in complete contrast to their Birmingham cousins, found little favour in such a vehicle, which saw very little use. The wagon was built in 1903 by the Metropolitan Amalgamated Railway Carriage & Wagon Company at their Saltley, Birmingham, plant and registered with the Midland Railway (registration No. 42188). The dimensions as registered differ from those painted on the side of the wagon, an unusual feature which may have been done for publicity purposes and the wagon shown to other prospective buyers before it was delivered. It was fitted with the Hunt & Shackleford patent hopper door mechanism, designed by Mr Hunt of the City of Birmingham Gas Department and Mr Shackleford of the wagon builder. The livery appears to be a red body with white letters shaded black.

Birmingham Central Library

Sivewright Bacon of Leeds and Nathaniel Attrill of Chesterfield.

On the Departments own admission its railway wagon fleet was in very poor condition in the late 1930s and as there were only around 100 wagons in use, an annual consumption of some 200,000 tons would equal 400 to 450 wagon loads a week. Bearing in mind that many short journeys were involved to and from the supplying collieries, and based on other users whose wagon turn-around times are known, it is suggested that between ten and fifteen percent of the supplies were carried in Corporation wagons. The balance would have been carried in wagons owned by collieries, railway companies or the contractors. There are no records of wagons being hired. In 1939 the fleet would have been pooled, with the exception of the tank wagons. By products from the other works still required some tank wagons, however, as the Corporation was in negotiation with Hurst Nelson in 1947 for new wagons, which did not eventuate. There are some interesting records of trading

from the latter as well as the gas works, coke was sold to Abbott of Birmingham and was exported to Copenhagen, coke was also sent to Norwich, and ammoniacal liquor from Giltbrook was purchased by Brotherton and Co. of Birmingham. During the first world war, the entire output of sulphur was sent to the Brotherton Works at Leeds by direction of the Ministry of Munitions, to make poisonous gas.

During the latter half of the nineteenth century, a lot of coke from the Nottingham Gas Works found its way to industrial users in the Birmingham area, in outright competition with the local product. The reason for its popularity was not difficult to ascertain, it was cheaper to buy the coke in Nottingham and transport it to Birmingham than to buy it from the local gas works!

MODELS : None

OSBORNE & SON

OSBORNE & Son appear to be a small coal merchant based in the east end of London, with their depot at West Ham South, on the former Great Eastern branch from Stratford to Silvertown, which incorporated several industrial and dock railways.

In 1930 the company ordered two 12-ton side door wagons from the Gloucester Railway Carriage & Wagon Company and the unusual feature is the body colour, Sheffield Green. This appears to be unique among railway wagon liveries and for the benefit of modellers, what has been learned about it from the most reliable source is presented here. It is suggested that it is a lighter shade than Emerald Green, and was revived in the 1960s by the Ford Company as a standard colour for their 1966 to 1968 models. The closest match that could be found was Dupont 8268L, No. 98256. However this does not guarantee that this colour is the same as the 1930 Sheffield Green!

Other wagons for Osborne came from W. R. Davies in October 1930 (No's 7 & 8), and Roberts in October 1937 (No's 1-6).

Being based on the former Great Eastern in the east end of London, coal supplies would have most likely come from the Doncaster or Mansfield areas via Whitemoor. Therefore these wagons would have been seen only in a limited area.

MODELS : None

Illustrated *above* is one of the two wagons, No's 9 and 10, purchased in 1930 from the Gloucester RC&WCo. and registered with the LNER (Reg. No. 6313). It was painted 'Sheffield Green' with white unshaded letters and black vertical ironwork. Small lettering at bottom right reads '**HEAD OFFICE - 54, ETHEL ROAD,** *Custom House, London, E.16. Phone Albert Dock 2022*'. No. 11, *below*, was one of two supplied in July 1942 (No's 11 & 12) and whilst having full livery was finished in grey. It has an end door and is fitted with disc wheels. *both GRC&WCo.*

PEASE & PARTNERS Ltd

THE Thorne Colliery of Pease & Partners, located near Doncaster, was one of the shortest lived large collieries in that area. Its owners were heavily involved in the coal trade of Durham and Northumberland, owning 14 collieries and a huge battery of coke ovens and facilities for producing the traditional by-products.

Sinking of the Thorne Colliery commenced in 1909 after the company acquired the site, close to the former North Eastern Railway between Doncaster and Goole, near Thorne Station. Work was suspended a short time later, resumed and suspended again, and was not resumed until after the first world war. Work recommenced in 1919 and was completed seven years later, constant problems being encountered with underground water. In 1927 1,200 men were employed and the well known firm of D. K. Rea & Sons acted as Liverpool agents. At this time Pease and Partners were a substantial force in the coal trade, for they also owned T. & R. Bower Ltd, owners of the Allerton Main Colliery near Pontefract, Henry Stobart & Co. Ltd and Bitchburn Coal Co. Ltd, both of Durham. The company had a total of 438 coke ovens at its various pits, and also owned four ironstone mines in Cleveland. Sir Arthur Pease, the chairman, was also a director of the London & North Eastern Railway and of Lloyds Bank.

The Thorne Colliery produced household, gas, steam and manufacturing coal. It may be significant that the rail connection with the North Eastern Railway faced in the direction of the Humber ports with the anticipation that this would be the direction in which the bulk of the coal mined would be travelling, for shipments were made at both Goole and Hull for export and bunkering, in addition to domestic customers, including one contract for 48,000 tons annually for the County of London Electric Supply Co., who had been a long-time customer of the Pease collieries in Durham. Gas coal was also supplied to the Gorleston & Southern Gas Co.

By 1950 the Thorne Colliery was one of the largest in Yorkshire with a payroll of 2,700, the tonnage raised was not revealed but it is unlikely that it ever reached the 1.5 million tons that was originally proposed. Six years later it was closed after perpetual difficulties with underground water, only 29 years after it opened. There have been proposals to re-open the colliery since, with the attraction of a nine-feet thick seam of best Barnsley bed coal – but, this is over 900 yards below the surface, and although preliminary work is believed to have commenced once and the proposal was revived only recently, the Barnsley hards have not been disturbed since 1956.

Pease & Partners, unlike most Northumberland and Durham

Charles Roberts & Co. Ltd built over 1,500 wagons for Pease and Partners, mainly for the Thorne Colliery or their subsidiary T. & R. Bower Ltd but that illustrated is not one that is recorded as such. It was built in 1928, and is thought to have been a sample wagon lettered for the company for approval before an order was placed. If these were the circumstances, those responsible were justified in congratulating themselves when the orders started rolling in. The eight-plank wagon has side, end and bottom doors. It was painted red with white letters unshaded and black ironwork. Italic letters at bottom right read *'Empty to Thorne Colliery, LNE.'*.

courtesy HMRS, AAR116

coal owners, operated a substantial fleet of standard twelve-ton wagons which would have been used mainly for coal deliveries outside of the immediate area, building several in their own wagon shops at the West Colliery at Crook, Durham. Others were supplied by outside builders as detailed below:

24.05.1906	892-911	Harrison & Camm	20T NER 6714-6733
10.01.1923	962-993	Charles Roberts	12T NER 15191-15222
15.08.1923	39-55	Charles Roberts	20-ton Tank wagons
	70-77	Charles Roberts	20-ton Tank wagons
			NER 10615-10622
04.1927	1142-1491	Midland	12T NER 13168-13517
07.1927	892-1141	Cambrian Wagon Co.	12T NER 12815-13064

Also built in the West Colliery shops were several wagons for the subsidiary company T. & R. Bower of the Allerton Main Colliery near Pontefract in Yorkshire. These were standard 12-ton wagons outshopped in 1924 and numbered 1003 to 1011, registered NER 11557 to 11565. All but two of the tank wagons lasted long enough to be taken into the ownership of the National Coal Board.

Further orders were placed for the Allerton Main Colliery in 1922 with Charles Roberts: fifty ten-ton seven-plank coal wagons numbered 912 to 961 painted black and measuring 15ft 6in. x 7ft 0in. x 4ft 0in. with side, end and bottom doors, and a further forty 12-ton eight plank wagons numbered 962 to 1001 also painted black and measuring 16ft 0in. x 7ft 5in. x 4ft 7in., again with side, end and bottom doors.

For the Thorne Colliery, the first indication of a supply of wagons came on December 7th 1927, when a minute in an LNER book which referred to the supply of registration plates recorded that Charles Roberts had notified of an impending order from Pease & Partners for 75 wagons. It appears that a sample wagon had already been provided before the order was placed. A further minute dated March 23rd 1929 reported a request for 900 registration plates for wagons for Pease & Partners, this, it will be noted, was after the first 169 of what was to be a total order for 1,334 wagons had been delivered as follows:

DATE	NUMBERS	QTY.	REGISTRATION NO'S.
24.01.1928	872 to 890	19	LNER 1658 to 1676
11.05.1928	1849 to 1941	93	LNER 2567 to 2659
10.12.1928	2016 to 2044	29	LNER 3258 to 3286
12.12.1928	2045 to 2091	47	LNER 3289 to 3335
11.01.1929	1703 to 1798	96	LNER 2084 to 2178
	1799 to 1848	50	LNER 2280 to 2349
25.06.1929	2092 to 2191	100	LNER 4026 to 4125
04.07.1929	2192 to 2291	100	LNER 4166 to 4274
	2292 to 2391	100	LNER 4267 to 4366
	2392 to 2541	250	LNER 4371 to 4519
	2542 to 2546	5	LNER 4528 to 4532
11.01.1930	2547 to 2746	200	LNER 5278 to 5477
25.03.1931	2747 to 2816	70	LNER 5666 to 5735

Additional to the above, included in the order were 175 wagons for the Allerton Main Colliery, 174 of which were numbered 1201 to 1374, registered LNER 5831 to 6004, the additional wagon presumably a sample wagon which had been sent for approval and retained. The delivery was completed on May 23rd, 1930. The wagons delivered in 1923 to 1927 and registered as the North Eastern Railway were included in that railway's Wagon Register books, and may have borne registration plates of that company. The LNER continued to issue separate sets of registration numbers for each constituent company until the beginning of 1927, when a new series and a new Register were introduced. Therefore duplications were possible unless the pre-grouping names were retained. At the time the Charles Roberts works must have been very busy, as large orders for the Carlton Main collieries and Henry Briggs were also in progress.

A solitary model of the Thorne wagon has been produced as a limited edition, and it is suggested to railway modellers that its use be restricted to the post-1927 period, Yorkshire area and the main lines and predominantly mineral lines between Doncaster and London, although they are known to have been sent to both Oxford and St. Albans.

MODELS : Bachmann/Rails of Sheffield

READING GAS Co. Ltd

READINGS third gas works, and the second to be rail connected, opened east of the town in 1888. The second works, in Kings Road, had received its coal over the internal sidings of Reading's famous Huntley & Palmers biscuit factory whereas the new works were provided with high and low level branches from the London & South Western/South Eastern Railway Joint Line, to which the GWR had access. Since some coal came via the Great Central line, the Gas Company had dealings with all of the Big Four. The 1888 works made good use of the Thames and the Kennet Navigation for tar and liquor shipment but there was no gas coal or coke by water after the 1860s.

In 1919 most coal was received from the Yorkshire coalfield, with some supplies from North Wales and the Potteries. The Yorkshire coal was supplied by local contractor Baker Bros from the Barnsley Main Colliery, and its most likely route would

have been via Annesley, Woodford and Banbury. A further source was Aldwarke Main Colliery near Rotherham which would have taken the same route, as did the 5,000 tons contracted for with the Great Western Coal Company from the Newton Chambers collieries near Barnsley.

The London coal merchant Peake, Oliver and Peake also had a contract for Apedale coal from north Staffordshire for 2,000 tons per annum, this was the only gas coal contract that this company handled as the general sales agents for that colliery. Coal from Ruabon in north Wales was supplied through local agents C. & G. Ayres and transported via the Great Western from pit to gas works, and the same contractor also handled coal from the Clay Cross collieries in Derbyshire.

By 1931 additional sidings for the gas works had been laid by the Southern Railway and coal contracts for 66,000 tons had been awarded as follows:

In the 1920s and 1930s Charles Roberts built several batches of new wagons for the Reading Gas Works, No's 101-110 were registered by the GWR in November 1925, No's 112 (illustrated)-116 were registered in December 1928 and No's 120-121 in June 1935. No. 112 is a standard eight-plank wagon with side and end doors and brakes both sides and measured internally 16ft 1in. x 7ft 7in. x 4ft 7in. It was painted black with plain white letters.

courtesy HMRS

CONTRACTOR	TONNAGE	ORIGIN
C. & G. Ayres, Reading	10,000	Ruabon (North Wales)
Baker Bros, Reading	7,000	Barnsley Main (Yorkshire)
T. Cash & Co, Birmingham	7,000	Markham Main (near Chesterfield)
	11,000	Yorkshire Main (near Doncaster)
Stephenson Clarke, London	10,000	Rothervale (near Rotherham)
	2,000	Bolsover (near Mansfield)
E. Foster & Co. Ltd, London	4,000	Elsecar (near Barnsley)
	3,000	Glapwell (near Chesterfield)
Rotherham & District Colls Assn	5,000	Aldwarke Main (Rotherham)
	5,000	Dalton Main (Rotherham)
	2,000	Kilnhurst (Sheffield)

In later years, C. & G. Ayres' contract was divided between Ruabon and the Smithy Wood Colliery near Barnsley, and Staffordshire coal was restored with supplies coming from Chatterley Whitfield. The above suggests that apart from coal from the Potteries and Ruabon, the majority of supplies were obtained from Yorkshire and the northern part of the Derbyshire coalfield, for which the most direct route to Reading was via the former Great Central as far as Woodford, where the Great Western would have taken over via Banbury and Didcot, although some could have been worked via the Midland Railway main line to Brent and transferred to the Southern at Feltham.

The company had a small fleet of wagons, which could have travelled to any of the above sources but most of the coal would have been carried in wagons belonging to the collieries and contractors listed above. In 1919 the contract for wagon maintenance previously held by Harrison & Camm of Rotherham was transferred to Wagon Repairs Limited of Birmingham. The fleet numbers quoted were 51 to 62, 65, 66 and 81 to 100, all coal wagons, and 67 to 80, which were described as coke wagons. Some of the coal wagons were described as being of fourteen-ton capacity.

That the gas works owned at least fourteen coke wagons suggests that their travels were not only to the collieries but also would have been seen carrying coke to local destinations, possibly as far away as Basingstoke, Marlow, Didcot and Swindon, as well as smaller stations en route.

The gas works was the origin of the episode described in *Private Owner Wagons: A First Collection* during the engine drivers strike of 1919 when the local locomotive foreman showed remarkable dedication and enterprise in driving a gasworks locomotive to the SECR sidings and with the Reading Station Master acting as fireman, drove a train of ten coal wagons back to the gas works, an act recorded with great appreciation in the gas work's minute book. As well as being fireman the Station Master probably also set the road and did the signalman's job as well.

MODELS : None

RUDGE BROWN & Co.

The wagon illustrated was built by the Midland company at its Washwood Heath, Birmingham, factory about 1915. It has seven planks, side doors only and brakes both sides. The body colour appears to be red with white letters shaded black and with black ironwork.

P. Coutanche collection

THIS company, based in Birmingham with an office in John Bright Street and depots at Monument Lane, St. Vincent Street and Camp Hill, was typical of the average sized coal merchant in a provincial city with a fleet of around fifty wagons and a turnover of some 40,000 tons of coal a year. The company would have traded with Warwickshire, Cannock Chase and South Derbyshire collieries as well as the Madeley Wood Colliery in Shropshire, the Blackwell Colliery in Derbyshire and the Highley Colliery near Kidderminster. Coke was purchased from the Birmingham Gas Works and the Blackwell coke ovens.

The company owned at least one coke wagon (No. 55) and in 1939 hired six 10-ton wagons from the Gloucester company.

The company also had a limited industrial trade, slack coal was loaded regularly at the Madeley Wood Colliery for the Buttington brickworks, and two small spot orders were obtained from the Bedford Corporation Electricity Department for coal from the Warwickshire Coal Co's Kersley Colliery near Coventry.

The range of the wagons would have been limited to the above areas.

MODELS : None

SALT UNION Ltd

THE company is still in existence today and most admirably, has deposited much of its photographic archive to the County Archives in Chester. It was in that county that much of its industry was located and the ample supply of natural salt in the immediate area provided the basic raw material upon which its business was built.

Incorporated in its works at Winsford was a power station, which required a constant supply of coal delivered in the company's own wagons. This was most likely obtained from nearby coalfields, such as north Wales, the Potteries or Lancashire.

Another Salt Union works was at Stoke Works, a short distance south of Bromsgrove on the Midland Railway main line between Birmingham and Bristol. The vintage industrial complex, bearing a different name, is still prominent beside the railway.

It was at Stoke Works that the company ran its own wagon building and repair shops, where new salt vans and open wagons were built. No records of the wagons built there have survived, but in the lineup of three wagons of indeterminable age and origin outside the works they may be represented.

The Stoke Works, in the late 1890s, used some 2,000 tons of coal a week, obtained from local collieries, one known source was Highley near Kidderminster, others would have been Cannock Chase and those around Cradley and Stourbridge. The coal wagons, which were identified as allocated to Stoke Works or Cheshire, would have been limited to those areas. Those used for the carriage of salt would have been the vans or other wagons reserved for such traffic.

MODELS : some Salt Union vehicles available from Powsides.

Taken at the Stoke Works sidings late in the nineteenth century, three wagons of considerable vintage are shown in the foreground. That nearest the camera, No. 136, has four wide planks and a top through plank, side doors only and raised ends, as has the wagon furthest away, its number obscured. That in the middle, No. 344, is of slightly more modern design with five planks, including a top through plank and side doors only. The company had its own wagon shops at Stoke Works which not only maintained the wagon fleet, but built new wagons and salt vans. There is insufficient information in the surviving records which would indicate if these wagons were actually built there. *Salt Union Limited Archives*

A view of one of the company's numerous Cheshire plants alongside the Shropshire Union Canal with a lineup of several wagons loaded with small coal, typically power station fuel. The photograph is insufficiently detailed to decipher the lettering on the wagon sides, but the top line of 'Salt Union Ltd' is reasonably clear. They appear to have grey bodies with white letters. Note that the wagons photographed in Cheshire do not carry the company emblem on their doors. *Salt Union Limited Archives*

This Sherwood Colliery wagon, No. 6089, is something of a puzzle as it does not fit into any of the known number sequences. It is likely that it was supplied secondhand from Hurst Nelson of Motherwell. Close study of the registration plate suggests an original registration in 1911 or 1917. It is suggested that this was a sample wagon sent by the builder for approval (something not unusual at the time) and painted in a 'workshops' livery which may not have been carried by the wagons in actual service: other photographs of Sherwood wagons suggest that they were painted red. The wagon illustrated has side, end and bottom doors and brakes both sides. The livery appears to be a light grey body with white letters shaded black and with black vertical ironwork. *courtesy HMRS, V1389*

SHERWOOD COLLIERY Co. Ltd

THE Sherwood Colliery, a short distance to the south of Mansfield Woodhouse Station on the former Midland Railway, was opened around 1904 and immediately established a wagon fleet with the purchase of 100 wagons from Harrison & Camm Ltd. The colliery produced manufacturing and steam coal, the distribution of which was mainly in the southern half of the country. together with local industry.

By the outbreak of the first world war the company had taken over the two collieries of the Hucknall Colliery Co. Ltd (not to be confused with the New Hucknall Colliery Co., which was actually at Huthwaite, some five miles away) at that village. Hucknall Torkard No. 1, was about a mile to the west of the village and served by the Midland and Great Northern railways, which were in 1899, joined by the Great Central, whose London extension passed nearby. It is interesting to note that the new Great Central main line ignored other collieries in the immediate vicinity, such as Bestwood and Linby, yet ran a spur into one of the Hucknall pits.

Hucknall Torkard No. 2 was situated close to the village centre and served by both the Great Northern and the Midland, giving access to the vast marshalling yards of Colwick (Great Northern) and Toton (Midland) from which mineral trains were despatched to London and all parts of the Midlands and East Anglia.

In 1931 the Sherwood company made another acquisition, the Kiveton Park Colliery Co. in Yorkshire, on the main line of the former Great Central between Sheffield and Worksop. This colliery produced mainly steam and manufacturing coal and its acquisition gave the Sherwood company access to the industrial markets of Yorkshire and Lancashire.

It is fortunate that a sales ledger has survived from the Kiveton Park Colliery; this shows that its coals were distributed to concentrated markets, it appears that all sales were funnelled through a small number of large coal contractors and factors. Kiveton Park coal was represented in London by Peake, Oliver and Peake; J. R. Wood; Montagu Higginson; Hoare, Gothard and Bond; Hinchliffes and Wm Cory. Austin of Cambridge was a solitary client from that part of the country, while in Sheffield its clientele was a roll call of the heavyweights of the trade there, Stevenson; Black; Jackson; Longbottom; Longbotham; T. W. Ward; Hallamshire and Barkby Joliffe. Kiveton Park coal was sold in Bolton by J. B. Scholes; in Manchester by Thrutchley, Beswick, Dutton Massey, Montagu Higginson and John Heaton; and in Liverpool by J. P. Higginson, Montagu Higginson and Dutton Massey; in Leeds by Cawoods; and in Bradford by Smith, Parkinson & Cole. It was exported through Hull and fired the locomotives of both the LMS and LNER.

In the 1930s the three Nottinghamshire pits produced a million tons a year and Kiveton Park lifted 700,000 tons annually. The company had a constant export market, in 1913 through Hull alone Sherwood shipped 50,000 tons, Hucknall 7,000 tons and

Kiveton 41,000 tons.

It has been relatively easy to trace the company's wagon fleet for the first few years as they were all registered with the Midland Railway, whose records have survived:

Mar. 1904	1-100	Harrison & Camm	43439 to 43538
Dec. 1904	101-200	Thomas Moy	44704 to 44733,
			44823 to 44892
Mar. 1905	201-400	Harrison & Camm	46426 to 46625
Mar. 1906	401-700	Thomas Moy	49475 to 49774
Apr. 1907	701-850	S. J. Claye	53730 to 53879
June 1907	851-875	S. J. Claye	53980 to 54003
June 1907	1001-1036	Hurst Nelson	54004 to 54040
June 1907	1037-1200	Hurst Nelson	54041 to 54204
June 1907	876 to 1000	S. J. Claye	54257 to 54381
Nov 1907	1201-1230	Hurst Nelson	55971 to 56000
	1231-1500	Hurst Nelson	56001 to 56120
			56326 to 56475

Some subsequent wagons were registered with the Great Central, including No's 1600 to 1700 built by W. Rigley & Sons Ltd of Bulwell Forest, Nottingham and delivered in 1922. No's 3000 to 3049 were delivered from the Lancashire & Yorkshire Wagon Company in March 1924 and registered with the LMS (No's 92342 to 92391). 1701-1800 were built by Rigley and delivered between March and June 1924. 5000-5099 were again built by Rigley and delivered between December 1938 and February 1939. 5100-5149 were delivered in April and May 1939 and once more came from Rigley. All of these latter wagons were registered with the LMS.

A 1927 photograph of Toton Yard shows two Sherwood wagons in distinctly different body colours, No. 47 from the original Harrison & Camm order which appears to be red; and a wagon numbered 4018 of which the origin cannot be located. It has cupboard-style doors more commonly associated with Scottish wagons and may have come from one of the Scottish builders. The body colour appears to be grey.

The railway which formerly served the colliery was closed to passenger traffic in 1968, but was one of those revivals in which the Nottinghamshire County Council in conjunction with local councils and other interested bodies were highly influential and was reopened for passenger traffic in 1993. Today, under the appropriate name of 'The Robin Hood Line', a thriving passenger service operates between Nottingham and Worksop, and puts the large town of Mansfield back on the railway map where it belongs.

Sherwood wagons were wide-ranging and would have been seen en route to London via the Great Central, Great Northern and Midland routes, in East Anglia and Lincolnshire and in the industrial areas of Notts, Derbyshire and South Yorkshire. When the Kiveton Park Colliery was taken over in 1931, it is assumed that in line with similar mergers the wagon fleets would soon have been intermingled.

MODELS (in red oxide) : Bachmann, Powsides, Cambrian/Holt Model Railways

A photograph of Toton Yard taken in 1927 (of which this is a fairly cruel enlargement) shows a Sherwood wagon which appears to be No. 4018 (part of the last digit is obscured) and in comparison with other wagons known to have been painted red nearby suggests that this one was actually painted grey. It also has cupboard style doors, quite unusual for wagons based south of Hadrians Wall. This makes the subject all the more interesting and intending modellers should take note. As this wagon also does not fall into any known sequence it may have been on hire.

In the same photograph is another Sherwood wagon, No. 47, a rare opportunity to view a Harrison & Camm product.

THE CAMBRIAN WAGON CO., LTD.
EAST MOORS ROAD
CARDIFF

A 20-TON HOPPER
Built for the British (Guest, Keen, Baldwins) Iron & Steel Co. Ltd.

Much of the expansion of the company away from its Oxford roots is told in its wagon fleet, and fortunately numerous photographs have survived and the selection reproduced indicates how widespread the company became over the years. Oldest is No. 3, photographed in September 1897 having been ordered the previous month. It was paid for over five years. It has five planks, full height side doors and internal diagonal bracing with internal dimensions of 14ft 6in. x 7ft 0in. x 3ft 1in. It was painted red with white letters shaded black and black ironwork and also shows the street address of the company. *GRC&WCo.*

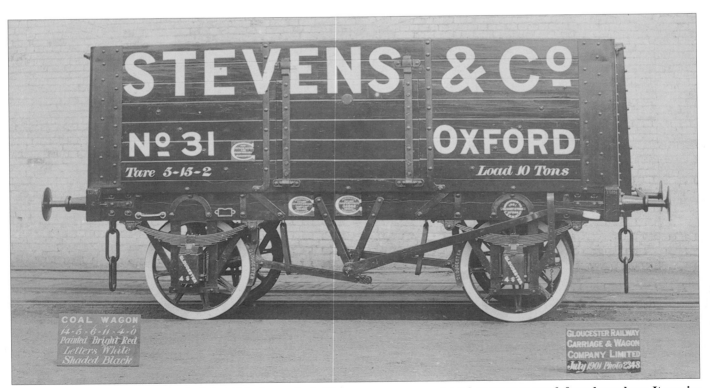

Wagon No. 31 was photographed in July 1901 when a single 10-ton wagon was purchased on seven years deferred purchase. It carries Gloucester No. 34852 and was registered with the L&NWR. Painted bright red, lettered in white with black shading and black ironwork. *GRC&WCo.*

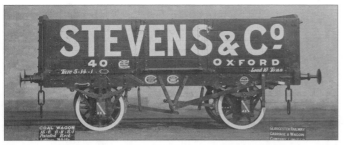

The next oldest wagon is No. 40, photographed in September 1902 by the Gloucester company, as were all of those illustrated. It is from an order for three wagons and has five planks with raised ends, full height side doors, inside diagonal bracing and brakes one side only. It measures (I.D.) 15ft 6in. x 6ft 11in. x 3ft 1in. and was painted red with white letters shaded black and black ironwork. *GRC&WCo.*

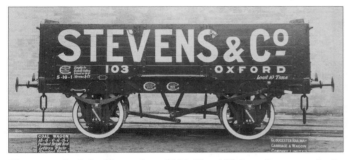

Photographed in November 1902 No. 103 has the same body dimensions as No. 40. It was one of four new wagons taken at this time. Body colour is once more specified as bright red. Lettering is white, shaded black and ironwork is black. Italic letters at bottom left read '*Empty to Exhall Colliery to load on a/c Stevens & Co.*'. Exhall Colliery was between Coventry and Nuneaton on the LNWR. *GRC&WCo.*

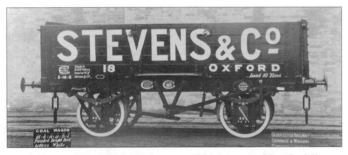

No. 18 photographed in February 1903 bore an identical livery and interestingly, came between No. 103 and 104! It was one of four wagons ordered the previous month. Empty instructions are the same as for No. 103. *GRC&WCo.*

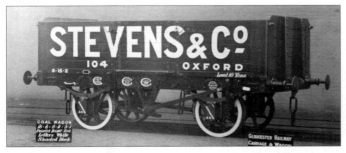

Further deliveries of new wagons took place in 1904 with an order for another ten, of which No. 104, photographed in January, was identical to No. 103 delivered two years earlier but without the empty return instructions. *GRC&WCo.*

STEVENS & Co.

STEVENS & Co. of North Parade, Oxford, was a substantial coal merchant with depots at the LMS yard at 8 and 9 Rewley Road, 6 Cornmarket Street, 93 Cowley Road, Grandpoint, Gosford and Kidlington in Oxford and distribution throughout the county and edging into adjoining counties and as far away as Warwickshire. By 1935 a branch office at 40 Earls Court Road, London had been established and further companies registered in Bournemouth, Cheltenham and Leamington Spa. In a rare sequence, the wagons purchased by the company over a period of almost forty years came almost exclusively from the Gloucester company, and, apart from the lack of empty return instructions, almost tell the company's history simply by examination of the photographs.

The company appears to have been founded around 1896 as this is when the first wagons were ordered from Gloucester RC&WCo. with a single 6-ton wagon being taken on 11 months hire. Gloucester was then patronised continually for both new and hired wagons. Subsequent orders for new wagons were placed in 1901 (1); 1902 (4); 1902 (3); 1903 (4); 1903 (10); 1904 (10); 1905 (2, 15-ton); 1924, (20, No's 550-569) 1926, (20, No's 570-589) and 1927 (23 No's 840-859 and 1000-1002). Although there are no records of wagons purchased elsewhere, there is a record in the LMS Wagon Register of 20 wagons built by S. E. Stevens of Doncaster for S. E. Stevens of Oxford numbered 820 to 839; registered 108988 to 109007. It is uncertain if these are for the same owner or if the entry was erroneous. The company also operated coke wagons, four ordered in 1903 included No. 45 emptying to the Oxford Gas Works, from which Stevens distributed coke over a wide area within Oxfordshire and adjoining counties. Seven secondhand wagons were purchased for cash in 1932.

Stevens patronised many collieries in the Warwickshire coalfield, in particular Arley, Griff and Exhall near Nuneaton and Baddesley near Atherstone. All were connected to ex LNWR lines, Baddesley by means of the noted incline from the colliery to the exchange sidings between Atherstone and Polesworth stations, over which the colliery's famous Beyer-Garratt locomotive worked regularly. The company also patronised the Donisthorpe Colliery and probably other Moira collieries in the South Leicestershire coalfield.

Around 1931 the company name was changed to Stevco Ltd., which was registered in both Oxford and Bournemouth, or alternately this was an independent subsidiary.

Looking at the known sources of supply and that many of the company's new wagons were registered with the LMS, much of its coal would have been routed through Nuneaton, Rugby, Bletchley and the former LNWR line from Bletchley to Oxford. That the main depot in Oxford was in the LMS yard reinforces that theory. If coal were sourced from Yorkshire or Nottinghamshire mines, this could have been carried to Oxford via the Great Central and Great Western through Banbury. The sphere of operations of Stevens' wagons would not necessarily be restricted to the routes from Oxford to the above coalfields, and considering the size of the company, it is also possible that it acted as a factor and sent wagon loads to small coal dealers in nearby towns and villages and into neighbouring counties, including Warwickshire, Berkshire, Gloucestershire, and Buckinghamshire.

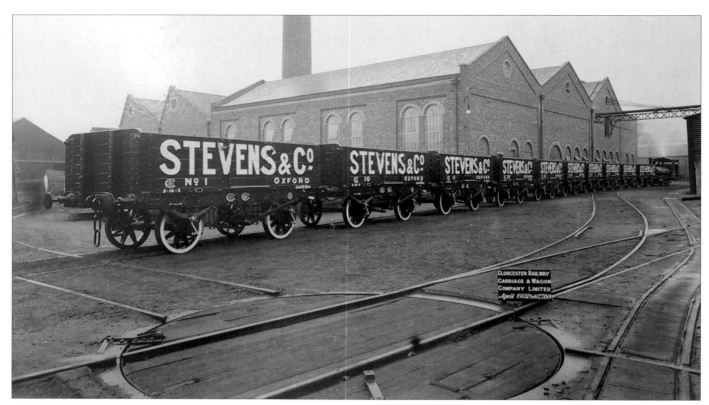

The above rake of ten wagons was photographed at the wagon works in April 1903. Wagon numbers discernible are 1, 10, 11, 20 and 25. *GRC&WCo.*

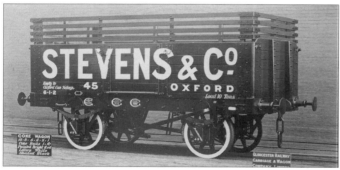

In 1903 an order was placed for four convertible coke wagons of which No. 45 is an example. These were five-plank wagons with side doors only and raised ends, inside diagonal bracing and brakes one side. Additional coke wagons were No's 216 to 219 which were photographed in July 1904 (*below*). The dimensions of No. 45 were (I.D.) 15ft 6in. x 6ft 11in. x 3ft 1in. without coke rails, which added a further 1ft 10in. to the body height. All of these were painted bright red with white letters shaded black and black ironwork, italic letters at bottom left on No. 45 read '*Empty to Oxford Gas Sidings.*' whilst on the four below it reads '*Empty to Oxford Gas Companys Sidings.*'. *GRC&WCo.*

A solitary wagon, delivered in 1905, No. 301, shows the address as London. It also bore the same body colour and lettering as No. 103, except for the different address. *GRC&WCo.*

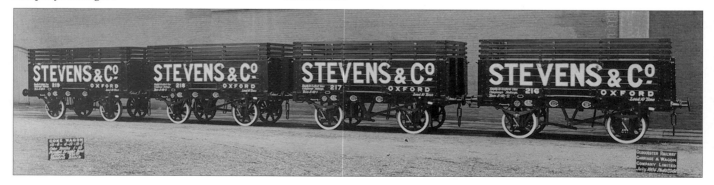

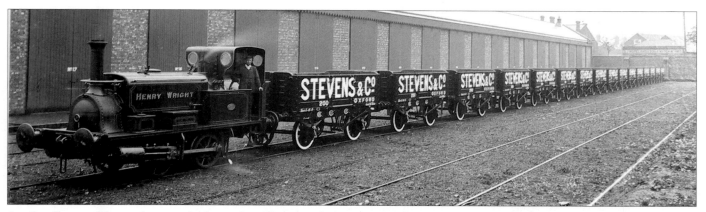

Another lineup of Stevens' wagons in the yard at Gloucester in August 1904 with sixteen new wagons, No's 200-215, behind one of the work's shunters (the other can be seen at the end of the rake opposite). *GRC&WCo.*

As well as new wagons Stevens & Co. took a number of short and long-term hires from Gloucester as this sample between 1896 and 1907 shows:

11 November 1896	s/h hire	11 months, 1 6-ton
13 October 1897	s/h hire	6 months, 2 6-ton
9 February 1898	s/h hire	1 year, 1 6-ton renewal
13 April 1898	s/h hire	1 year, 3 8-ton
8 September 1898	s/h hire	7 months, 1 6-ton
12 July 1899	s/h hire	5 years, 3 8-ton renewal
9 August 1899	s/h hire	1.25 years, 1 6-ton
11 October 1899	s/h hire	5 years, 2 8-ton
8 November 1899	s/h hire	3 years, 2 8-ton
11 July 1900	s/h hire	7 years, 3 8-ton
14 August 1901	s/h hire	7 years, 1 8-ton
12 October 1904	s/h hire	1 year, 2 6-ton, 2 7-ton
11 January 1905	s/h hire	1 year, 1 6-ton
8 March 1905	new hire	weekly, 1 15-ton
8 November 1905	s/h hire	6 months, 2 6-ton
13 February 1907	s/h hire	3 years, 6 10-ton
9 October 1907	s/h hire	6 months, 6 10-ton

MODELS : Powsides, Dapol/Osborne Models.

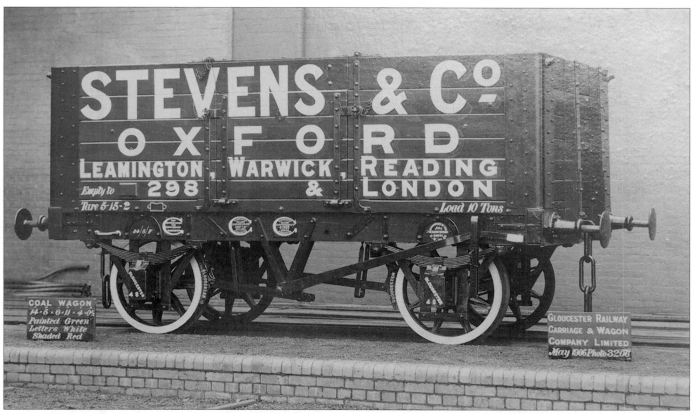

A complete departure was shown in a 1906-built Gloucester wagon, No. 298, which also shows the then existing branch addresses of London, Leamington, Warwick and Reading as well as Oxford. This was a six-plank wagon of more substantial appearance with side doors, a lift-over top flap door, inside diagonal bracing with internal dimensions of 14ft 6in. x 6ft 11in. x 4ft 0in. It also had a totally different colour scheme of a green body with white letters shaded red and black ironwork and which was, from the photographic evidence available, probably an isolated one. *GRC&WCo.*

103

A further wagon delivered in 1909 is No. 500, with seven planks, side and end doors but brakes one side only. It measured (I.D.) 15ft 6in. x 7ft 4in. x 4ft 0in. and was painted bright red with white letters shaded black and black vertical ironwork. Lettering at bottom left reads 'DEPÔTS - WARWICK, LEAMINGTON, KENILWORTH, READING & LONDON.'. Registration was with the L&NWR.   *GRC&WCo.*

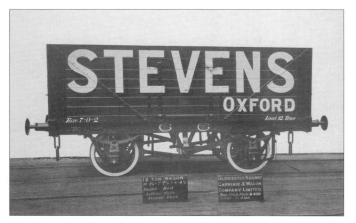

Moving into more modern times, this un-numbered wagon was built in 1924 and was a standard RCH side door seven-plank wagon with brakes both sides. The LMS wagon register tells us that it was from a batch of twenty numbered 550 to 569 (registration No's 93141 to 93160). The solitary Oxford address has been revived, although the other branches were still in business. Measuring (I.D.) 16ft 1in. x 7ft 7in. x 4ft 4in. the paint description this time was just 'red' with white letters shaded black and black vertical ironwork.   *GRC&WCo.*

The next order was for 20 wagons, No's 840-859, placed in 1927. Illustrated is No. 853 of 12 tons capacity with side doors only and brakes on both sides. Dimensions and livery were as the example above.   *GRC&WCo.*

In the 1930s the company trading name was either changed to **STEVCO**, or a subsidiary company under this name was established. Whichever, the photograph of wagon No. 868, purchased secondhand from Gloucester in 1931, is proof. Again it was a seven-plank wagon, of recent vintage but this time with side and end doors and brakes both sides.   *GRC&WCo.*

Other wagons, numbered from 901 up and of considerably earlier vintage were also supplied lettered '**STEVCO**'. Again being secondhand no livery details are recorded but a red body with white letters shaded black and black vertical ironwork is suggested. The body colour appears lighter in the photograph but this effect was most likely due to different types of film being used. Note the oval plate between the end stanchions.   *GRC&WCo.*

The twenty-ton all steel wagon No. 1001 is another Gloucester product and is from an order for three wagons placed in 1927. They were numbered 1000-1001 and were registered with the GWR in June 1927.   *GRC&WCo.*

104

TAR DISTILLERS Ltd

TAR is a by-product of making coal gas or coke and was distilled to produce a bewildering range of chemicals. At first tar was the only source of naptha and creosote, the remainder being burned as fuel. Later, refined tar became the binder of choice for dust-free roads (tarmacadam), pitch made 'patent fuel' possible and creosote was the standard preservative for timber. Motor spirit was improved by adding benzol (a 'British Made' product) whilst most plastics and many domestic and medicinal products from mothballs to carbolic, dyes, perfumes and powerful drugs like M&B 693 all derived from coal tar. Many tar products were exported, not least huge volumes of creosote to preserve railroad 'ties' in the USA. In time of war, toluol from coal tar was added to that stripped out in the gas works and nitrated to make TNT.

Tar Distillers Limited of 44 Grosvenor Place, London S.W.1 operated such a plant at Pinxton, on the Notts/Derbyshire border, beside the premises of Notts & Derby Coke & By-Products Limited opposite the Brookhill Colliery of the Pinxton Colliery Co., between Pinxton and Kirkby-in-Ashfield and on the Nottinghamshire side of the county boundary. This was an independent company, of modest size, and outside the combines. In 1938 they bought 12,212 tons of crude tar for distillation, falling to 4,465 tons in 1944.

It is thought that the wagons did not travel far from their home base, as there were many sources of raw material nearby. However, on occasions this could be contradicted as in the late 1890s by-products from the gas works at Birmingham were sent by rail as far afield as Leeds and Manchester, and one shipment to Glasgow was recorded.

The plant was connected to the Midland Railway connecting the Erewash Valley route with Kirkby and still in use for freight traffic. On one side was the tangle of lines which served the sprawling Pinxton Colliery and a short distance away to the east was the Kirkby Bentinck Colliery of the New Hucknall Colliery Co. Today the M1, running on a high embankment near the A38 junction between Pinxton and Kirkby, offers a grandstand view of the heavy industry which now occupies the site of the colliery, the coking plant and the tar distillery.

Tar Distillers Ltd. patronised G. R. Turner of Langley Mill for their known wagon fleet, commencing with ten tank wagons No's 1 to 10 delivered in 1922, followed closely by a further eight numbered 11 to 18. Two rectangular tank wagons were purchased in 1924, numbered 19 and 20.

MODELS : None

The wagon illustrated is one of ten cylindrical tank wagons built in 1922 by G. R. Turner Ltd of Langley Mill, numbered 1 to 10 and registered with the Midland Railway (registration No's 83428 to 83437). A further eight similar wagons were built in 1924, numbered 11 to 18 (registration No's 85116 to 85123). They had dimensions of: tank barrel 17ft 5in. long by 5ft 7in. diameter on a wheelbase of 10ft 6in. The tanks were painted black with white lettering and the underframe appears to be red. The wagon number is repeated on the tank end. Small italics at bottom right read: *'Regd Office, 44 Grosvenor Place, London S.W.1.'*. Two rectangular tank wagons, No's 19 and 20, were purchased from the same manufacturer in 1924 and registered with the LMS (No's 93995 and 93996). They measured 15ft 9in. x 7ft 4in. x 3ft 4in. and were probably also painted black with white letters.

Midrail Photographs

No. 015 was a 10-ton hopper wagon fitted with the manufacturer's own patent discharge apparatus, and was photographed at the works following a repaint after being hired to the City of Birmingham Gas Department for twelve months. Unfortunately the photograph is undated and although it was fitted with brakes both sides, the design dates to the nineteenth century and is not unlike those used in quantity by the Birmingham Gas Department, whose records of wagon hires, although extensive, are insufficiently detailed to determine its age. Painted black with white letters. *Midrail Photographs*

G. R. TURNER Ltd

THE wagon building firm of G. R. Turner Limited, of Langley Mill, on the border between Derbyshire and Nottinghamshire, and in the industrialised heart of the Erewash Valley, dates back to 1868 when a small local engineering firm produced custom-made bits and pieces for local collieries, wheelbarrows and started repairing railway wagons.

Production of new wagons commenced around 1875 and on the very first page of the first Private Owner Wagon register book of the Midland Railway are details of wagons built by Turner for the Hardwick Colliery. The company was one of the small to medium sized wagon builders whose products were sold mainly in the nearby coalfields but some went to south Wales and others to East Anglia and London. The company also manufactured and fabricated steelwork and mining equipment and were an early specialist in all-steel wagon construction which led to a successful export trade.

Railway wagon construction ceased in 1958 and the company was eventually acquired by the United Steel Companies Ltd, producing fabricated steelwork and general engineering. Like many institutions large and small which manufactured railway wagons, the works have been closed and the site of eight acres is occupied by a road haulage company.

Both wagons illustrated are lettered as sample wagons which could be sent to any prospective purchaser for trials.

MODELS : None

The second wagon, un-numbered, is a twenty-ton wagon designed for iron ore traffic and is of a type that such companies as Clay Cross and Sheepbridge owned in considerable numbers to carry ore from their various quarries to the blast furnaces of the Erewash Valley. The wagon has a registration plate of 1927. 420 were built for Stanton between 1927 and 1934 and a further 167 during the second world war. It appears to be painted red oxide with white letters shaded black. *Midrail Photographs*

106

This battered, war-torn No. 1354 is typical of the way most Private Owner wagons ended their lives, unkempt, unidentifiable, but still running. From the brackets on the top plank it may have originally been a convertible coke wagon with seven planks and side, end and bottom doors. Judging from the running number it was built around 1923 and may have come from a batch built by Hurst Nelson. From the look of the track it was not photographed on a main line! *collection of the late Bernard Holland, per Mark Smith*

WATH MAIN COLLIERY Co. Ltd

WATH Main was a very large colliery situated amidst what would have been a perpetual sea of private owner wagons, it was beside the Wath Concentration Yards of the Great Central Railway, through which was funnelled a huge amount of coal traffic, much of which was eventually hauled through the Pennines via the Woodhead Tunnel, bound for the industry of Lancashire and export from Liverpool and Birkenhead. Apart from the Great Central, the colliery was also connected to the Midland Railway main line between Sheffield and Leeds, and the Wath Branch of the Hull & Barnsley Railway, giving direct access to Hull, Lancashire via the Woodhead route, the Lincolnshire ports and to London via both the Midland and Great Central routes. The colliery shipped 106,000 tons of coal via Hull in 1913: this was carried not only along the direct Hull and Barnsley route, but also by the Great Central via Hexthorpe and the Midland to Normanton, where the North Eastern took over.

Even in the 1920s Wath Main was originating over 600,000 tons of coal a year, between 11,000 and 12,500 tons a week, or an average of 250 wagon loads a day. Its coking plant also despatched approximately 3,300 tons of coke per week plus the usual by-products: Patent Oven Coke, crude coal tar and crude benzole. It consisted of 30 Simon Carves ovens with a capacity of 170,000 tons per annum. This was distributed all over the country, principally in the Lancashire and Yorkshire areas and particularly the heavy industry around Sheffield and the Scunthorpe steel mills, and in the early part of the twentieth century substantial quantities were sent to Birmingham.

Wath Main gas coal, of which around 165,000 tons a year was mined in the late 1930s, was distributed throughout the country, as far away as Ambleside in Westmorland and Shoeburyness on the Thames estuary, to Wallasey on the Wirral peninsula, Bognor Regis on the south coast , Tavistock in Devon, and throughout the Midlands, East Anglia, and Lincolnshire.

It is fortunate that most of the company's trading records have been preserved pre-1916 and from 1937 onwards and an interesting comparison can be drawn by comparing the markets for Wath Main coal in 1910, when very little gas coal was produced, and 1939, when the trading pattern had changed considerably.

In 1910, regular contracts were negotiated to supply the following customers during just one month! This list is incomplete, as the original is faded and the writing is very small and at times indistinct: Tom King, Ashton-under-Lyne; Edward Bannister, Grimsby; Spinners Coal Co., Stalybridge; Outhwaite & Sons, Burnley; North Lincolnshire Iron Co., Scunthorpe; Walter James, Derby; J. Taylor, Ashton-under-Lyne; Halifax Industrial Society, Halifax; C. J. Lord, Settle; S. Sidebottom, Manchester; Tinker Bros, Holmfirth; Ormerod, Rochdale; Holwell Iron, Melton Mowbray; T. Boston & Sons, Birmingham; J. Baker & Co., Rotherham; Hall & Sons, Macclesfield; Craven Lime Co., Skipton; J. Hargreaves, Leeds; Walter Thorpe, Glossop; Calico Printers Association, various locations; Stalybridge Corporation, Stalybridge; Higginson, Liverpool; Burns & Lindeman, Hull; C. W. Organ, Desborough (Northants); W. Milburn & Co, Hull; Lutze & Co., Grimsby; A. Johnston, Hull (for export to Sweden); Great Northern Steam Fisheries; Great Central Railway; Humble & Ramskir, Doncaster; A. Lacey & Co., Hull; Oldham Equitable Co-op, Oldham; Montagu Higginson, Liverpool; New Cransley Iron & Steel, Kettering.

This is in addition to the regular deliveries to the company's domestic coal accounts. The interesting features are the large deliveries to traders at the Humber ports, and a large amount of coke sold to the Birmingham merchant T. Boston & Sons, who in one year ordered over 20,000 tons.

Moving on to 1939, many contracts were held to supply gas coal through Evesons (Coal) Ltd of Barnsley, a branch of a company based in Birmingham which on an average month purchased 15,000 tons of coal from Wath Main alone, was responsible for the marketing of over half of its gas coal production and which is featured elsewhere in this volume. One look at the contracts for June 1939 will show a wide variety of clients in many parts of the country. Of specific interest are the contracts with Montagu Higginson & Co. of Liverpool for delivery to Andrew Weir & Co. (owners of the Bank Line of steamships) and also to MacAndrews, another ship owner. Montagu Higginson are also known to have contracted for the supply of Wath Main coal to the Blue Star line of refrigerated cargo ships.

In 1939 the days of the coal burning cargo ship were well on the decline, and these particular contracts are of more than usual interest as the export and bunkering trade had declined to the extent that only around 50,000 tons a year were being sold for these purposes at all seaports.

Other major clients in 1939 were: Arthur Fellows, Rotherham; Rafferty & Watson, of Hull (who took over the Wath Main office at that port when it was vacated by the colliery company); the LMS railway; the LNER; Lancashire Cotton Mills, who placed a single order of 8,000 tons through Humble & Ramskir; Longbotham & Co, Sheffield; Modern Transport, Leeds; E. A. Stevenson, Sheffield; Walter Thorpe, Glossop and Stockport; Yorkshire Tar Distillers, Kilnhurst; Fletcher, Leeds; Smith Parkinson & Cole, Bradford; Stanton Ironworks, Holwell, Leicestershire; New Cransley, Kettering; Thomas Black, Sheffield; Shap Granite, Shap; Stephenson Clarke (gas coal to

Godalming, Croydon and Bognor Regis, the latter by ship from east coast ports); J. E. Cowcill, Barnsley; John Heaton, Manchester; Rickett Smith, (deliveries to Chesterfield); Stewarts & Lloyds, Bilston; Settle Limes, Settle; Thrutchley & Co., Liverpool; Cawood Wharton, Leeds; Hadfields, Sheffield.

There is not much evidence of London traffic, or for that matter outside of gas coal contracts, any manufacturing or household coal traffic outside of the general area of Lancashire and Yorkshire. James of Derby was a regular customer, as were Lamont and Warne of Poplar; Rickett Smith of London; Stonehouse and Cory of Newcastle; J. C. Abbott of Birmingham for coke only, and the industrial area centred on Scunthorpe in Lincolnshire. Over the years, the centre of gravity of Wath Main coal consumption had changed considerably.

In December 1939 coal sales had totalled 38,074 tons inland and 4,685 tons export and bunkering, whilst the coking plant contributed another 10,000 tons.

The 1939 pattern of gas coal distribution shows that apart from the clients served by Evesons (Coals) Ltd, which are described elsewhere in this volume, other customers were the gas works at Harrogate, Radcliffe, Oldham, York, Tavistock, Ilkley, Leeds, Croydon, Howden, Blackburn, Skipton, Bridlington, North Middlesex, Lancaster, and the Gas Light & Coke Co. of London. These were contracted by Stephenson Clarke, Modern Transport, J. E. Cowcill, John Heaton, Fletcher & Sons, Rafferty and Watson, E. Foster & Co., Humble and Ramskir, and Cawood Wharton.

The Wath Main wagon fleet is referred to only casually in the company records, but from it we can learn that in 1910 100 new wagons were ordered from Thomas Moy of Colchester and a further 100 wagons were on hire each from the Lincoln

No. 1320, which may have come from the same order as No. 1354, was built by Hurst Nelson and delivered, it appears, in 1923. It has seven planks and side, end and bottom doors. Livery was a red body with white letters shaded black, in italics bottom right are 'LM&S&L&NE'. No. 1320 has black ironwork, No. 1354 probably also had at one time. *courtesy HMRS, ABP 933*

108

Engine & Wagon Co. and the British Wagon Co. Other wagons were hired at various times from H. G. Lewis of Cardiff and coke wagons were hired from Thomas Moy. A Moy advert shows Wath Main No. 1010 in 1912. Lettering is much the same as for 1354 except that the number is over the door as per 1320. A purchase of fifty second hand wagons for yard use from C. Clough and Co., wagon builders, Atlas Works, Mansfield is also recorded. The wagons would have been very widely distributed, carrying gas coal into most parts of the country. In 1925 two were photographed outside the Birmingham gas works, where, surprisingly, the Wath Main Colliery, and indeed Evesons, did very little business.

In 1939 at pooling day, the fleet was 1,161 wagons owned and 456 on hire; not particularly significant for such a large colliery, which suggests that almost a half of its products were carried in wagons belonging to its customers.

MODELS : Dapol/Midlander

The fifteen-ton wagon No. 5 was one of ten built in 1904 by G. R. Turner of Langley Mill and registered with the Midland Railway (registration No's 46101 to 46110). It has two doors on each side and bottom doors. Of nine-plank construction and measuring internally 21ft 1in. x 7ft 6in. x 5ft 2in. and with a wheelbase of 12ft 0in., it was painted grey with white letters shaded black and black vertical ironwork. The small plate on the right of the wagon is the builder's plate. The light colour of the running gear may have been for photographic purposes only.

Midrail Photographs

WELLINGBOROUGH GAS LIGHT Co. Ltd

THE site of the gas works of this Northamptonshire town and important railway centre, strategically half way between the marshalling yards of Toton and London can still be seen on the down side of the former Midland main line a short distance on the London side of Wellingborough Station. The source of its coal suggests that the Midland Railway, and later the LMS, was responsible for the carriage of most of it all the way from colliery to gas works.

Wellingborough's second gas works opened in union Road in 1904 and, unlike the 1833 site, were rail connected. The 15-tonners were part of the new arrangements. Contracts for its supply in 1929 were awarded as follows:

CONTRACTOR	TONNAGE	COLLIERY OF ORIGIN
Dalton Main Colliery	1,000	Dalton Main
Old Silkstone Colliery	2,000	Old Silkstone
E. Foster & Co. Ltd	1,000	Denaby
Midland Coal and Coke Co.	1,000	Apedale
Modern Transport	1,000	Elsecar
	1,000	Wharncliff Woodmoor
United Steel Companies Ltd	5,000	Rothervale
Midland Coal and Cannel Co.	1,000	Monckton
Stephenson Clarke	1,000	Birley
	1,000	Rockingham

All of these collieries except Apedale, in Staffordshire, were located in Yorkshire, Birley (near Sheffield), Old Silkstone and Elsecar (both near Barnsley) on the former Great Central lines of the LNER and the balance on the former Midland lines of the LMS. Denaby was served by both. By 1932, coal was still sourced from the same suppliers and contractors. However, in 1930 an allowance was made in the invoiced price for the gas works supplying their own wagons, while the 1932 contracts were most specific in quoting for the use of colliery or contractors' wagons only. This does not, however, imply that the gas works no longer owned their own wagons.

The company patronised, from surviving records, the wagons works of G. R. Turner of Langley Mill exclusively, the first order being placed in 1904 for ten fifteen-ton wagons. Like most of their ilk, these were never really successful and most were broken up or disposed of in the 1920's. In 1924 a further order was placed for thirty 12-ton wagons which offered more proven longevity and the first ten also duplicating the running numbers of the fifteen-ton wagons.

Therefore with the supply of coal consistently originating from similar sources, the scope of the operation of these wagons would be limited to trips between the gas works and the collieries listed above, via the Midland main line to Toton and beyond, with short interludes on the LNER in Yorkshire. The company also hired wagons from Wagon Repairs Limited, whose Wellingborough works were only a short distance away.

MODELS : No. 29 Powsides

The second wagon, No. 29, is from an order placed with G. R. Turner in 1924 for thirty wagons numbered 1 to 30 and registered with the LMS (registration numbers 94561 to 94590). It is an RCH standard seven-plank wagon measuring 16ft 1in. x 7ft 7in. x 4ft 4in. with side and bottom doors and brakes on both sides. The wagon appears to have a medium to dark grey body with white letters shaded black and black vertical ironwork on the corner plates and door hinge straps only as illustrated. *Midrail Photographs*

THE WERFA DARE COLLIERY Co. Ltd

THE colliery was opened around 1875, and was connected to a branch of the Great Western Railway Vale of Neath line from Abernant to Merthyr and to the west of the Merthyr Tunnel. There was also a privately owned incline railway or tramway which connected it to the Cwmbach colliery, which provided a connection to the main Vale of Neath line to Pontypool and its connections to the seaports of Newport and Cardiff.

It was not a particularly large colliery. In 1938 production was 70,000 with a workforce of 238. The distribution of coal is unknown as no records of the independent colliery appear to have survived.

MODELS : None

The oldest of the wagons illustrated is No. 369, a Gloucester product of 1915. It has seven planks, side and end doors, brakes both sides and was registered with the GWR. Internal measurements were 15ft 6in. x 7ft 4in. x 4ft 2in. and it was painted black withwhite letters. Italic letters above 'ABERDARE' read '*Agents - Greenslade & Williams. Cardiff.*' and at bottom left read '*Empty to Aberdare. G.W.R.*'.   GRC&WCo.

No. 801 was built in 1923 by Gloucester RC&WCo. and was part of an order for fifty wagons. It was of 12-tons capacity, seven planks, side and end doors and brakes both sides. It measured internally 16ft 0in. x 7ft 4in. x 4ft 2in. Livery is again a black body with white letters. Italic letters at bottom left read '*Empty to Werfa Sidings, Aberdare, G.W.R.*' and on solebar '*For Repairs advise Colliery.*'. *GRC&WCo.*

No. 803 was photographed in July 1942 and was among the last wagons to receive a full livery before the utility style took over completely. It was part of an order for five 13-ton wagons numbered 801-805. They were registered by the LMS.   *GRC&WCo.*

Supplied in March 1934 by Gloucester RC&W and, although turned out like a new wagon, it is actually of some considerable age and was sold secondhand, possibly an ex-hire vehicle and, although the registration plate is illegible, it probably dates back to the early part of the twentieth century, before the seven-plank wagon became almost universal. Finished in red with white letters shaded black and black vertical ironwork. The company also operated wagons with a more conventional livery, one is illustrated in A. G. Thomas's *The Modellers Sketchbook of Private Owner Wagons*, Vol. 1, where the business is described as colliery agents. *GRC&WCo.*

H. O. WHITE

THE Banbury coal merchant H. O. White, of 43 Bridge Street, occasionally hired wagons from the Gloucester company, who were also responsible for wagon repairs. The wagon illustrated is one that was rejuvenated in 1934, three hired wagons were returned in 1939 and six ten-ton wagons hired in their place.

The Derbyshire Fumeless Coke advertised on the wagon side came mainly from the coke ovens at Winning 'A' Colliery of the Blackwell Colliery Co. Ltd, near Westhouses on the Midland Railway a short distance to the north of Alfreton. The route to Banbury would most likely be via Toton, Washwood Heath, Bordesley and Leamington to Banbury. The style of painting of the wagon, with the product advertised with such prominence, is unusual and only a few coal merchants thought it necessary to promote their product rather than be identified by name.

MODELS : Osborne Models

WILLIAMS & SONS

ERNEST Williams was first listed as a coal merchant in 1927 at Canal Bank, Daykin Avenue, Witton, on the former LNWR line between Birmingham and Walsall, best known today for its proximity to the Aston Villa football ground.

The business was apparently not a particularly large one, and the advertising on the body of the solitary known wagon may even imply that only coal for steam lorries and wagons was supplied. This would also include steam rollers and traction engines, which at the time were still widely in use, although the internal combustion engine was making steady inroads.

The wagon has been included principally for its almost unique advertising.

It is possible that two 12-ton wagons, No's 3 and 4, built by the Midland RC&WCo. in February 1924 for 'Williams & Sons, Birmingham' were also for this owner.

MODELS : Powsides

Wagon No. 1 in the fleet of this small merchant was acquired as a rebuilt wagon from the Gloucester RC&WCo. in 1926. Unusual is the lettering on the top plank, which suggests that the owner specialised in supplying the owners of fleets of steam lorries. The source of the coal, according to the empty return instructions, suggests otherwise, the best reputations for steam raising coal in the Birmingham area were the collieries of Kingsbury and Haunchwood, in Warwickshire. Painted black, lettered white with a white top plank and black letters. The italic letters at bottom left read '*Empty to Cannock Chase Colliery. Brownhills, L.M.S.*'. Note particularly the telephone number on the wagon body. *GRC&WCo.*

WILLINGSWORTH IRON Co. Ltd

THESE works were located at Wednesbury, on the former Great Western main line between Birmingham and Wolverhampton, much of which has now been given over to the Birmingham Light Rail system. The company had its own private sidings on the west side of the line between Wednesbury and Bradley & Moxley stations, and also had access to the Gospel Oak Branch of the Walsall Canal. On the opposite side of the Great Western main line was a chemical works and this appears to have been connected by an internal railway system. The entire area, according to an Ordnance Survey map of the 1920s, appears at that time to have been a vast wasteland of abandoned collieries, quarries and industrial sites. A short distance away were the Swan Village Gas Works of the City of Birmingham and the Monway Iron and Steel Mill, served by both the Great Western and the LNWR South Staffordshire Branch.

Their immediate neighbours were far better known, Wagon Repairs Ltd, the Patent Shaft & Axletree Company and Chance & Hunt. In other words, a concentration of both heavy and offensively aromatic industry which today would be the source of much attention from the environment groups. The ironworks and the Patent Shaft & Axletree companies were related, the latter was well known as a subsidiary of the Metropolitan Amalgamated Railway Carriage & Wagon Co. Ltd, but it was not generally known that the ironworks were also a part of that company, having been acquired in 1909 following the financial failure of the previous owners.

Among the raw materials received at the Willingsworth private siding were coal, coke, limestone and iron ore.

In 1909 the company purchased fifty large hoppered wagons from the former Oldbury Works of the Metropolitan Company. Numbered 250-299 they were registered in two batches by the GWR, No's 250-270 in April 1909 (Reg. No's 378-398) and No's 271-299 in June 1909 (Reg. No's 409-437). They were registered as carrying 20 tons which suggests, from the capacity of the wagon, a fairly heavy load for its size. Therefore iron ore is a possibility, although coke cannot be ruled out.

MODELS : None

The impressive No. 292 was built by the Oldbury Works of the Metropolitan Amalgamated Railway Carriage & Wagon Co. in 1909 as part of an order for fifty such wagons, numbered 250-299. It has side and bottom doors, ten planks and brakes one side only and was registered by the GWR to carry 20 tons. The registration number appears to be 490. The wagon has dimensions of (I.D.) 15ft 11in. x 7ft 8in. x 5ft 9in.; overall height above rail level was 9ft 11in. on a wheelbase of 9ft. 6in. It appears to be painted a deep red with plain white lettering and black ironwork The rectangular notice above the tare weight refers to it being a new wagon on its first journey and not to be loaded above four tons.

Birmingham Central Library

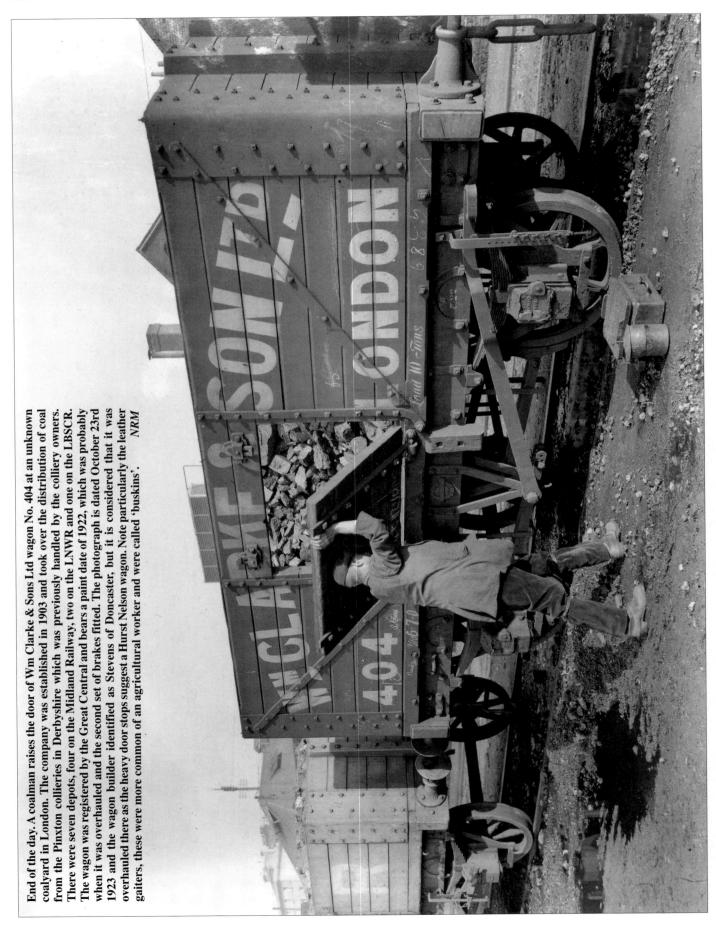

End of the day. A coalman raises the door of Wm Clarke & Sons Ltd wagon No. 404 at an unknown coalyard in London. The company was established in 1903 and took over the distribution of coal from the Pinxton collieries in Derbyshire which was previously handled by the colliery owners. There were seven depots, four on the Midland Railway, two on the LNWR and one on the LBSCR. The wagon was registered by the Great Central and bears a paint date of 1922, which was probably when it was overhauled and the second set of brakes fitted. The photograph is dated October 23rd 1923 and the wagon builder identified as Stevens of Doncaster, but it is considered that it was overhauled there as the heavy door stops suggest a Hurst Nelson wagon. Note particularly the leather gaiters, these were more common of an agricultural worker and were called 'buskins'. *NRM*

114

AT THE COLLIERY AND THE COALYARD

THE coal wharf and the landsale depot, as well as the railway siding and the local goods yard, have all passed into the history books and are remembered now as part of the lexicon of both the railway system, the city, the town and the village where coal fuelled the furnaces of the industrial revolution, the gas works that lit the streets and, once, the houses, the power stations that provided the electricity, lighting and heating, the bakery, the mill, the brewery, the factory and the fireplace at home.

The coal merchant was part of life as much as the milkman, the baker, the local Co-op and the postman and paper boy. His infrequent visits when coal was rationed during the war were welcomed with the traditional greeting 'I'll put the kettle on' as three one-hundredweight bags were emptied into the 'coalhouse' by muscular arms and broad shoulders in a cloud of dust. In mining areas the collier received his one ton allocation in bulk by lorry. It was dumped in his driveway or in the street from where all hands that could be mustered, together with whatever buckets, shovels and wheelbarrows could be assembled, combined to move it to its place of storage.

To trace the transportation of coal from colliery to railway siding up until the time of wagon pooling – and the loss of choice of the retailer and merchant – the following cumbersome and laborious procedure was followed. The example given is for coal transported by train – that which was moved from colliery to retailer by means of the canal network was quite different. Here the carrier was an independent canal boat owner,

such fleets as those of Fellowes, Morton & Clayton and Samuel Barlow ascending to folklore status, trading from collieries in the Warwickshire, Cannock and Leicestershire coalfields in such a traditional fashion into the 1950s.

A coal merchant with his own wagon fleet in Kent or Sussex buys his house coal from, say, a colliery in Nottinghamshire. An empty wagon is labelled to be sent to that particular colliery. It is picked up by a local goods train and taken to the nearest marshalling yard, where it is then assembled into another train bound for an interchange point or yard on the outskirts of London. From there it is forwarded into a transfer freight to the yard of the railway which serves the colliery. Occasionally the preferred routing instructions are painted on the wagon side, but more likely the originating railway would have to work out which route the wagon was to take, from a standard laid down in a directory. Or his last order may have arrived in a colliery owned wagon and this is then returned empty to its owner. If the coal merchant deals through a coal factor, it is the factor who would be notified of the despatch of the wagon and who would be responsible for notifying the colliery that it had been despatched, along with any others that were bound for the same colliery.

In turn it is marshalled into another train of empty coal wagons, all bound for collieries in the Nottinghamshire area, to a further marshalling yard on the outskirts of Nottingham, such as Colwick (LNER), Annesley (LNER) or Toton (LMS). Here it is re-marshalled into a train of around fifty empty wagons, all

The coal sidings at Ferme Park in North London *c.*1907 on the Great Northern Railway. Shunting is in progress at the south end of No. 3 Coal Sidings with loaded wagons being sorted, possibly for onward transmission. The view clearly shows the iron strips attached to the tops of the wagon sides and ends from which it can be seen that the wagon on the engine has full-height side doors. Note the shunters armed with their poles at the ready.

courtesy John Alsop

bound for the same colliery which could have come from fifty different stations and owners. On arrival at the colliery these wagons are shunted into the designated empty sidings, and the wagon handbrakes pinned down. These sidings were often situated on a slight down gradient so that gravity would take over when the wagons were to be rolled under the screens for loading.

Collieries that worked several seams may have only worked particular seams on nominated days or limited the loading of certain grades of coal to a particular time. Many had a special raised siding which did not pass under the screens but ran straight into the grading plant, these were to be loaded with hand selected large lumps, the most expensive that the colliery produced. Often it was reserved for special customers.

The coal merchant, or factor, in the meantime, would have sent the following letter to the colliery company:

'We have despatched this day our wagon No. 24 to you and would be obliged if you would load it with small cobbles and return it to us as soon as possible'.

The colliery would pass this order on to a sales clerk who would raise an internal order form detailing the client, wagon number and type of coal that was required. This would then be passed on to the employee in charge of incoming wagons, who would have been responsible also for labelling it back to the owner before it was loaded. Many owners, and most large users, had pre-printed two sided labels and all that was needed was to reverse the wagon label, which would not only show the destination but also the grade of coal which was to be loaded. The wagon label was then a directive. This required some juggling by the colliery shunting engine when the train of fifty empty wagons may have been for several different grades. But with wagon pooling, this, and many other costly and labour intensive practices, was to end.

Once loaded, the wagon would have been weighed and the tare and gross weight, wagon number, owner and destination passed on to the colliery office by a 'weighman' so that the merchant could be billed, and an invoice posted as confirmation that his order had been filled and the coal was on its way.

In the colliery office, as in the office of a coal factor or that of a large coal merchant, back in the days of manual accounting, large and heavy ledgers rested on rows of high, sloping benches, and an army of clerks writing in impeccable copperplate in ink,

Somewhere on the London & North Eastern a 2-8-0 heads a train of loaded wagons mainly belonging to Messrs Cleeves, Ault & Fowell of London, an example of a batch of coal heading from the colliery to the capital.
courtesy Paul Karau

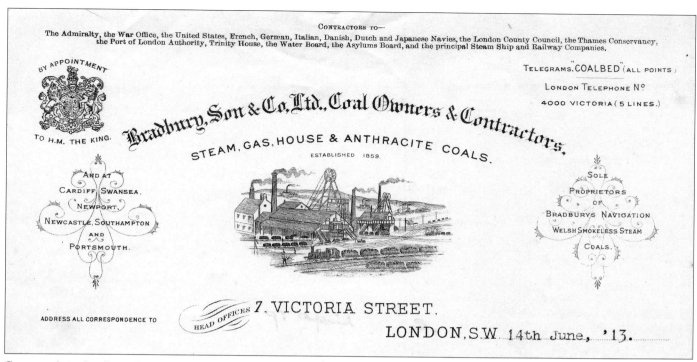

Company letterheads, such as this for Bradbury, Son & Co. Ltd who are featured on page 22, often give an amount of useful information on the business. In this case details of their government orders, both home and abroad, and their main London contracts are listed. From it can also be gathered the date the business was started, their head office, regional offices and some of their products. The contents of the letter can also be of interest, in this case it was a quotation for the supply of Bradbury's Merthyr best Welsh smokeless thro' at 24s. 6d. per ton delivered f.o.r. (free on rail) to Redruth Station for South Crofty Ltd, a tin mine at Carn Brea.

Ian Pope collection

calculated mentally several columns of figures and with remarkable accuracy balanced whole sets of ledgers across and down. Records were kept of full and empty wagon movements, wagons out of service for whatever reason, tare and loaded weights, invoices and receipts, accounts from various railway companies for transportation, credits and debits, all originating from a single document provided from the weighbridge. The larger operators, whose wagons emptied to a marshalling yard rather than an individual colliery, maintained offices and personnel, as well as coal supplies and both loaded and empty wagons which could be despatched at short notice to any colliery or customer where they were needed at that yard.

The battalion of clerks were usually supervised by a Chief Clerk, often a tyrannical individual with many years service and who would not tolerate the slightest transgression or even an ink blot from an often denigrated, but highly skilled, profession whose degree of mathematical and written skills have now been forgotten along with the pen nib, the inkwell and blotting paper.

All of these paperwork procedures today would be carried out by a single keyboard entry into a computer from a similar source document and in turn the client would be invoiced, the wagon would be traced, statements forwarded and payments recorded all at the push of a button on a keyboard. Those traditional clerks took great pride in their work, their trade has disappeared in the same manner as the typist, stenographer, office boy, the Station Porter and the Mechanical Horse delivering railway parcels.

The loaded wagon, meanwhile, would then be included in a train of up to fifty wagons, which was taken by an engine that had brought empty wagons earlier in the day and the entire process of marshalling, re-marshalling and eventual delivery to the owner was repeated. Photographs of wagons in service often show large numerals chalked on their ends. If the example of the procedures at the Toton Marshalling Yard between Derby and Nottingham is taken, this was written on the wagon by the foreman in charge of the hump shunting, a direction for the men armed with the traditional shunters poles where to uncouple, and to the signalmen working the points in the manual days which siding the wagons were bound for.

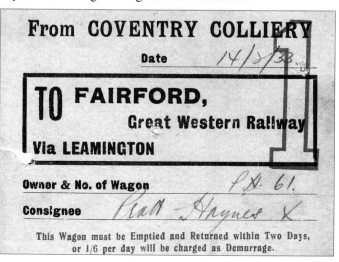

From COVENTRY COLLIERY

Date 14/8/38

TO FAIRFORD,
Great Western Railway
Via LEAMINGTON

Owner & No. of Wagon   P.X. 61.

Consignee   Pratt Haynes

This Wagon must be Emptied and Returned within Two Days, or 1/6 per day will be charged as Demurrage.

And the time taken for this transport cycle? From the south coast to Nottinghamshire and back, fourteen days. Therefore a ten-ton capacity wagon, which when well filled with large coal may have only carried nine tons, could be expected to make a maximum of 26 journeys a year, carrying 234 tons of coal in total. Todays transport manager would expect that much to be carried in a 20-ton capacity bulk carrying truck in a single week.

Wagon pooling was to end all of this. Once the wagons had been loaded, they were carded to wherever coal was allocated, in the beginning coal destined for large users was loaded into wagons that were totally unsuitable for those with their own unloading devices. The numerous teething troubles that surfaced took some time to resolve. Gas works were supplied with coal that was unsuitable for gas making and large coal was sent to power stations, and as an interim solution essential services such as gas works, power stations, munitions works and factories were allowed to buy their coal through their regular contracted collieries and suppliers until the controlling bureaucracy acquired sufficient knowledge of what coal to send where.

On the wagons arrival back at the coalyard, landsale depot or siding its handbrake would be pinned down. If its contents were to be delivered in bulk a lorry with its tailgate removed would be backed up, the wagon door would be dropped into the back of the lorry and around a ton of coal would immediately fall out and be shovelled off the now horizontal door. The lorry would be driven slowly forward, the door would drop, releasing a few more lumps,

and then driven alongside the wagon so that loading could resume. For manual unloading, the smaller eight- and ten-ton wagons were vastly preferred by the smaller coal merchants if they were to be unloaded by hand, as the door was of the same height as the wagon.

Seven-plank wagons with conventional doors meant that the coal had to be heaved over the much higher wagon side or as the load diminished, shovelled to the door and then handled again. Some seven-plank wagons had folding or lifting upper doors so that the entire height of the wagon was open and these were much easier to unload. That such fleets as Charringtons had a large number of such wagons is an indication that they were unloaded in the manner of a ten-ton wagon, that is, through the open doorway and manually. These procedures continued in their traditional way and were unaffected by either wars or wagon pooling, but a limit was set on the time that a wagon was stationary and penalties in the form of demurrage were charged if it was not emptied within a certain time.

At the landsale depot where the author served his 'apprenticeship' as a small boy the driver did most of the loading with occasional assistance from a labourer, out in the open in all weathers, and each three-ton lorry was expected to do four 'runs' a day delivering colliers' coal in one ton lots in the adjoining village, usually large cobbles which arrived in yard wagons until wagon pooling, when any wagon could be used. With large coal, often an implement like an enlarged garden fork with eight tines more closely spaced was used, as it was

A Cardiff coalyard with two wagons belonging to Pensom & Beavis, both unfortunately unidentifiable with regards to number or maker. The two lorries, and the horse dray are all signwritten for T. Pensom who can be found trading from 54 Partridge Road, Cardiff in 1938.

National Museums & Galleries of Wales

Coal being loaded in bulk and bagged for delivery at the landsale siding of the Birley Colliery near Sheffield. The lorry is typical of those that carried up to forty one-hundredweight bags on delivery rounds to small consumers, although the drop sides were not so common, except that it allowed both bagged and bulk coal to be carried.

Sheffield Public Library

easier to get into the coal until the wagon floor had been reached. Once loaded, a weighbridge confirmed the accuracy of the driver's judgement which was remarkable in that each load never varied by more than a few pounds in weight, for if the three-ton load was more than half-a-hundredweight over the driver was required to unload the excess on the spot. However, nothing was ever said if it was half-a-hundredweight short! Only bulk deliveries were handled, those households in the village which received a monthly ration of bagged coal were served from a siding several miles away where pooled coal from any colliery was sent, to be picked up by a carrier from a nearby village. So was the efficiency of the industry during the war!!

Twenty wagons of coal were emptied each week by this method. For a short time, the lorries were loaded under the screens and this increased the delivery rate dramatically, as if a modern-day time and motion study expert had been employed. It could have eliminated one delivery vehicle, saved several gallons of rationed petrol and dispensed with the labourer, but true to tradition such a drastic change in procedures did not last for long, the intrusion of the coal lorries under the screens frequently interrupted the loading of railway wagons and the old manual method was soon reintroduced.

Seven-plank wagons were hard enough to empty manually but even harder was any wagon which had an uneven floor. By the end of the war most of them were so decrepit that this was a regular feature and a steel plate was placed over the wagon floor near the door so that it could be used as a shovelling plate. Occasionally a stray non-pool wagon found its way into the landsale yard, one that comes to mind was a Stanton Ironworks low sided twenty-ton tube wagon, which had already resisted all attempts to load twenty tons of coal into it. When a wagon was completely empty, at 'our' landsale depot it was always removed from the siding with the door still open, but this was, apparently, a practice limited to such facilities that were physically attached to a colliery.

Bagged coal was different. Coal sacks were made of heavy and thick jute with two large grab handles at the top and held a hundredweight each. One method was to prop up the wagon door on the horizontal with a stout pole and stand and shovel from that position. This practice was highly dangerous and forbidden in the more responsibly run coal yards. At one Nottingham coal yard a four wheeled cart was drawn up alongside the wagon door and coal was bagged until it was full. Then the coalman had a rest for a few minutes until an empty cart appeared from a completed delivery run. Carts were exchanged and the driver and coalman had very little rest but the real loser was the poor horse which was immediately hitched to a loaded cart and on its way in a few minutes. Some workers slowed down if they could get away with it so that when the empty cart arrived, its driver was obliged to help to fill the few remaining bags and at least the horse had a short rest.

In a one man, one cart business the horse was definitely better off. It was hot, dirty and very hard work yet some coalmen thrived on it and worked into their 70s. One man known to the author worked until he was almost eighty and after retiring was still active in his ninetieth year. Another, well past 70, rose at 4am in the summer, emptied two full wagons of coal, then retired to a farm and milked fifty cows before lunch.

Looking through a directory of the 1930s, when there were some 28,000 coal merchants in Britain, it is apparent that many such businesses were father and son operations, like many other trades, passing through generations of the same family. It is an interesting comparison that in 2003 there were just as many Indian restaurants in the country.

Typical of the smaller lorries used for bulk coal distribution, this two ton Commer of the early 1930s worked from the Dalton Main company's Silverwood and Roundwood collieries in Yorkshire. *Wakefield Collection*

Motor vehicles entered the scene early in the trade, they were reported carting coal from the Lawley Street Sidings to the Adderley Street Gas Works in Birmingham as early as 1907. When motor vehicles and steam lorries started to replace the horse in earnest, often an old cart was left in the yard as a platform and temporary storage for bagged coal, which was transferred to the lorry on arrival. Many contrivances were used to assist in filling coal bags, often cobbled together by the coal dealer and crude as they were, they usually worked. One method was to make an iron or wooden frame with hooks so that the bag could be suspended with its mouth open, and this was a great help for filling. One side was hinged, so that when the bag was full the hook was removed and the hinged arm lifted. Another method of bagging coal was into one-hundredweight sacks on the ground, usually from large bins into which wagons had been emptied, which then had to be lifted onto the cart or lorry. Some horse drawn delivery carts had huge wooden wheels around six feet in diameter, hence the need for a portable staircase or ramp.

Most coal yards were out in the open, but some of the big merchants had undercover accommodation in the form of a simple shed over a single track so that the weather was not allowed to interfere. At more modern yards conveyors were used to load lorries, some such systems incorporated a small elevated bunker which held around six tons, this could be designed to discharge into the lorry in bulk, or through a chute into bags. Following nationalisation and the concentration of coal handling facilities with something like 20th century equipment, many of the traditional methods and much of the hard physical work were banished forever. Facilities replaced included those where elevated sidings were provided so that coal could either be shovelled out into large bins, often made from discarded railway sleepers or released through bottom doors if the wagon had them. The North Eastern had always preferred this method, with 'cells' loaded from the top by hopper wagons.

Many coal merchants stocked several grades of fuel, the various grades, nuts, small cobbles, large cobbles, best house coal, anthracite and steam coal were separated into such bins and woe betide any coalman who unloaded coal into the wrong bin or delivered the wrong variety, for customers were sufficiently educated to know the difference, if not when it was delivered then as soon as it was put on the fire! That some unscrupulous merchants passed off inferior coal as better quality and were found out is reflected in the contracts of the Warwickshire County Council, who were the victims of such dishonesty to such an extent that they demanded a certificate of origin from the producing colliery for each delivery.

There was also a row of small buildings at each coal depot where the offices of each merchant was located. Here an excellent survivor is at Wakefield Westgate on the perimeter of the car park, which occupies the former site of the goods yard. Such offices contained only the very basic requirements, an old desk and chair, space for tools, limited usually to a supply of shovels and a solid ball-peen hammer to ensure that the most recalcitrant wagon door was released. There was usually a communal toilet, space for horse feed, stables and a weighbridge. The buildings and the weighbridge were invariably the property of the railway company and the merchant paid an annual rental. It is hard today to find an original example of such a coalyard, but one of the most outstanding examples of surviving goods depot architecture in the entire country can be found at Burton-upon-Trent, and although it is not immediately visible to passengers on passing trains, it is almost alongside the railway station, behind the magnificent Midland Railway Grain Warehouse, where one can find a block of coal offices in almost mint condition, a weighbridge together with its office, (now converted to a lunch shop), and a goods office. Although the towering Grain Warehouse has been gutted and converted into small factories, its external appearance, with the exception of some minor modern appurtenances, is still very much of the pre-grouping era and the entire setting is complemented by vintage lamps and a large area of cobblestones. In this often maligned town it is one of many classic examples of industrial archaeolog , many of which are connected with its long history in the brewing trade. The same principle of storage, large bins often constructed of old sleepers with old rails set in concrete as uprights, is used by sand and gravel merchants, whose materials now arrive by articulated tipper lorries, another means of eliminating hard work.

There were always disputes over short weight in wagons, few of which were acknowledged and admitted by the colliery of origin, loose doors and missing floorboards being the most common excuses if the shortage was in a wagon owned by the receiver, and pilfering en route a frequent explanation for a few hundredweight missing when the wagon was owned by the colliery. Unreliable weighing methods by some coal merchants who bagged coal at the railway siding or coal wharf and judged the weight of its contents by how full it was provided another reason for disputes over weight, a favourite excuse for covering up a few extra lumps on the delivery vehicle which were surreptitiously dropped off en route at an unscheduled location. Two instances are known where contracts were cancelled due to continuing disputes over wagon weights. Both involve the same Welsh colliery. One of these was reported in the anecdotes in *Private Owner Wagons: A First Collection*.

As the traditional coal merchant with his horse and cart or secondhand lorry and shovel disappeared following nationalisation and restructuring of the industry, his local clientele spread over a few streets were transferred to a larger and more mechanised dealer. But in a small way the tradition still lives on, for in the Leicestershire village where the author lives, coal is still delivered by lorry in bags, not the huge jute sacks of yesteryear, but 25-kilogram bags made from a tough synthetic fibre. Unwashed, with an overly high proportion of dust and slack, coal it may be called, but if we had delivered anything like this from Blidworth many years ago, a call would soon be forthcoming to take it back. What is called household coal today at least burns and produces that satisfying smell of smoke only coal can give.

But the coal wharf and the landsale depot have passed into history, overtaken by progress. In its day, it was so common that it, like the Private Owner Wagon, went unsung, unheralded and unphotographed. Only a handful of pictures survive, some in the form of postcards issued by coal merchants which showed either their delivery vehicles or their wagons. Fortunately a few have been found and used to illustrate this chapter.

WAGON REPAIRS Ltd

THE company was registered on March 5th 1918 at Rotherham with its registered office at Imperial Chambers, John Bright Street, Birmingham, specifically:

'to carry on in the UK or elsewhere the trade or business of repairing, rebuilding, reconstruction, painting, altering, converting, equipping, adapting, making fit for traffic, supplying and dealing with railway or other wagons, trucks, corves, carriages, trolleys, vans and vehicles, also a range of tramway and motor vehicles, and repairing wheels, axles and components.

To carry on in the UK the building and constructing of new railway and other wagons.

To build, establish, acquire, hire, rent, sublet, occupy, use, manage, carry on and deal with any factories, workshops, foundries, depots, mills, building, sheds, outstations, warehouses, wharves, erections, yards, railways, tramways, sidings, etc.'.

The driving force behind the company was Dudley Docker but from the beginning it is apparent that the company was supported in its intended trade by many of the major wagon builders, in particular Charles Roberts & Co. Ltd, of Wakefield, a director of which, Mr Duncan Bailey, was also a director of Wagon Repairs Ltd. In 1930, the goodwill and certain repair facilities of Charles Roberts were transferred to Wagon Repairs in return for a fully paid issue of ordinary and preference shares. Initially, the combined might of Charles Roberts, the Midland RC&WCo. of Birmingham, Hurst Nelson from Scotland, Metropolitan of Birmingham and the Gloucester RC&WCo. were the owners of this nationwide wagon repair facility.

The formation of a body such as Wagon Repairs was a long overdue consolidation by the various wagon builders, many of whom had repair depots scattered all over the country, a typical example being at Chester where there were four such depots, each owned by one of the companies which were to oversee the formation of Wagon Repairs Limited. Accordingly there was an immediate and substantial saving in the cost of the provision of such facilities where a degree of rationalisation could be effected.

Reference to the City of Birmingham Gas Department in *Private Owner Wagons: A First Collection* will give some indication of the chaotic state of the wagon repair and maintenance business at the time the company was formed, when 16% of its entire wagon fleet was out of service at one repairer alone, and when repair contracts were more or less awarded to the lowest priced bidder regardless of the original builder, a situation that resulted in the Department eventually building their own wagon repair shops, which in turn built several hundred new wagons. Ironically, this was only a few months after Wagon Repairs Ltd was founded in Birmingham itself.

The company expanded quickly. Immediately it was in operation, new business was generated. For example, the Reading Gas Works soon transferred wagon maintenance to Wagon Repairs Limited. It is almost beyond doubt that repair contracts held by the wagon builders who sponsored the formation of the company encouraged their clients to do likewise: indeed repairs disappear from Gloucester RC&WCo's books by June 1918.

By 1923 a considerable transformation in ownership was recorded. Without delving into the financial side of the company, a roster of its shareholders showed that Charles Roberts no longer held either preference or ordinary shares, but added to the original founding companies were the Birmingham Railway Carriage & Wagon Co., the British Wagon Co., S. J. Claye Ltd, Harrison & Camm, and the North Central Wagon Company, the latter being the most substantial shareholders with some 25% of the preference shares. By this time the company had been in business for five years and the cost of establishing works depots and purchasing plant and equipment resulted in accumulated losses of almost one million pounds. In that year a substantial reorganisation of capital amongst the wagon companies that were shareholders saw the financial holdings of each reduced by about 10%, and in 1927 following closure Harrison & Camm withdrew altogether. Soon afterwards the company took over all of the repair contracts for wagons owned by the short lived and controversial wagon finance and hire company H. G. Lewis & Co. of Cardiff and its associated L.W. Co. Ltd who had over 40,000 wagons out on simple hire. Repair contracts were also assumed from various other wagon repairers and builders, an arrangement with the Gloucester company was that 10% commission on the cost of repairs to any wagon for which Gloucester held the contract, was passed on and such an agreement was probably in effect with others also.

Already in 1920 a works depot was established at Stoke-on-

Trent and not long afterwards most of the important traffic centres in South Wales saw the arrival of Wagon Repairs Ltd. In 1921 the Birmingham Railway Carriage and Wagon Company were repairing wagons for several owners on behalf of the company at their Smethwick factory, although they were not a party to its initial formation. Some repair stations, such as Wellingborough, were of such substantial size with numerous sidings that a locomotive was required to handle all of the shunting. There are some records extant which show that a major repair contract was transferred, an example being a total of 482 wagons owned by Imperial Chemical Industries under three contracts, transferred from Gloucester between 1934 and 1936. This may have been encouraged by shareholding wagon builders, but there is reasonable evidence to show that other builders also encouraged the transfer of repair contracts and there is unquestionable evidence that Wagon Repairs also operated from within the premises of such builders as Claye of Long Eaton and the Lincoln Engine and Wagon Co.

Taken from trade directories in 1935, the location of the various depots and outstations throughout the country shows a selective network, although it is considered that the foregoing list is incomplete as directory advertising was inconsistent overall: for example, a large repair depot at Sandiacre, Derbyshire, obviously reflects the proximity of the Toton Marshalling Yards, yet no such depot was advertised for either Annesley or Colwick across the border in Nottinghamshire, although both were equal in importance. That only one depot was advertised in Birmingham is also questionable, a single location only, on the Great Western at Tysley, shared by several others, was recorded in that city but a contemporary Ordnance Survey map shows a further depot established, also on the Great Western, at Wednesbury. Also incongruous are, according to the directories, seventeen wagon repair organisations located at New England, Peterborough and not a single one at the Whitemoor Marshalling Yard at March.

WAGON REPAIRS DEPOTS

LONDON	Poplar Docks, Battersea
SOMERSET	Radstock
BRISTOL	St Phillips
GLOUCESTER	Lydney
LINCOLNSHIRE	Scunthorpe
DERBYSHIRE	Sandiacre; Whittington (Chatsworth Works)
LEICESTERSHIRE	Coalville, Leicester
NORTHANTS	Wellingborough, Northampton
WORCESTERSHIRE	Worcester
WARWICKSHIRE	Leamington
STAFFORDSHIRE	Smallthorne, Burton-upon-Trent
BIRMINGHAM	Tysley
HEREFORDSHIRE	Hereford
SHROPSHIRE	Ludlow
CHESHIRE	Saltney, Chester, Northwich
YORKSHIRE	Beighton, Alexandra Docks (Hull), Balby, Hexthorpe, Skipton
WALES	Swansea, Cardiff, Bridgend, Barry, Llanelly, Newport, Aberdare, Llanharan

(Source: *Kelly's Directories*, 1935/6)

The various works catered for any repair job from replacing a three-link coupling or brake block to completely rebuilding wagons damaged in shunting accidents, derailments or other serious causes, in direct contrast to some of the smaller and more remote 'repairers' whose kit could be limited to a shed, a wheelbarrow, a bicycle and a few tools. Contracts were entered into for the maintenance of entire fleets and this included periodical repainting.

In July 1936 major shareholders were The Gloucester Railway Carriage and Wagon Company, Metro-Cammell and its subsidiary Midland, both of Birmingham, Hurst Nelson of Motherwell, North Central Wagon Co. of Rotherham and Charles Roberts. In addition Leslie Boyce, the Gloucester chairman, was also a shareholder.

The company was a priceless asset in wartime with its facilities doubtlessly stretched to their limits: it survived nationalisation and continued to operate from its own and several wagon builders' premises throughout the country. With the state of goods rolling stock in the immediate post war years, there was never any shortage of work and the part that the company played in the rebuilding of the railway system during the aftermath was obviously just as vital and important as was the long overdue founding of the company at the conclusion of the previous world war. The comapny, although renamed, still exists.

No. 1306, was a Gloucester product delivered in 1943 and built under the wartime re-equipment programme as described in *A First Collection*. **The order was for a hundred wagons and these were delivered new to Penrith in Cumbria.** *GRC&WCo.*

Above and opposite top: **Three plates of the company from branches which were not directory listed! This can only be described as inexcusable for the Gloucester branch which was worked in conjunction with the wagon building works who were one of the founding companies of Wagon Repairs.** *Ian Pope collection*

METROPOLITAN RAILWAY

THE Metropolitan Railway on the north-western outskirts of London may be thought of as a long distance commuter system reaching out into the more desirable environs in the Chiltern Hills with an assortment of electric and steam hauled services radiating from Baker Street, London and partly entwined with the London Underground system, but all of those leafy suburbs also needed a supply of coal not only for domestic use, many of them also had small gas works that required a regular goods service and sidings were accordingly provided at many stations.

In addition the Metropolitan required coal for its steam locomotives and its power station at Neasden. Some of the power station coal came from the Kent coalfield but most originated in Nottinghamshire or Derbyshire and would have been worked via the Great Central main line which also served Neasden, and coal for the outlying parts of the system would most likely have originated from the same source. The designated point of transfer for coal arriving on the Great Central main line for other stations on the Metropolitan Railway network was Woodford and Hinton, well outside Metropolitan territory, but it could have been worked from there to a specific exchange point where there were adequate sidings.

Records of the Metropolitan Railway held at London Metropolitan Archives amongst the London Transport deposits include references to its coal contracts for both the power station and its locomotives and are detailed below, although in some instances they lack full detail.

CONTRACTS FOR NEASDEN POWER STATION
SIX MONTHS ENDING JUNE 30TH 1933.

Langwith Colliery, nutty slack	18,200 tons	21/6 per ton delivered
		9/1 per ton at pit
Snowdown slack	13,000 tons	20/2
		11/4
Blackwell slack	8,400 tons	21/-
		8/10
Manton Wood slack	5,200 tons	21/3
		7/8
Haunchwood slack	2,600 tons	20/-
		9/10

Two years previously the Snowdown Colliery in the Kent coalfield had been the biggest supplier with 52,000 tons per annum. This was sent by rail and routed around the western outskirts of London: there are references to the Great Western and Southern Railways allowing a reduced rate for their sectors of haulage. Langwith, Manton Wood, Warsop Main and Blackwell collieries were all in the Mansfield/Worksop area and served by the LNER and their contribution would have been transported to London by the former Great Central route. The Haunchwood Colliery was near Nuneaton and accessed by the LMS and this would have probably been worked via Nuneaton, Rugby and Willesden. There is no mention of coal factors involvement in the above contracts which leads to the conclusion that this was carried in colliery and railway owned wagons.

LOCOMOTIVE COAL

In 1927 the sole contractor for the supply of locomotive coal was Stephenson Clarke & Associated Companies Ltd and in that year 25,000 tons were delivered from the Ocean collieries in South Wales. By 1929 this figure had fallen to 15,000 tons. Prior to 1927 coal had been supplied from the Mansfield Colliery of the Bolsover Colliery Co., who also participated in supplies ordered frequently through the spot market, where orders were placed for both the power station and the locomotive fleet.

SPOT ORDERS RECORDED 1927

Stephenson Clarke	500 tons Blaenant; 500 tons Rhymney Valley; 5 wagons Nixons Navigation; 5 wagons Blaenant; (South Wales) 500 tons Warsop Main Top Hard; 1,000 tons Bestwood Main Steam; 1,000 tons Mansfield (Notts)
J. McElroy & Co.	500 tons Holly Bank slack (Cannock); 500 tons Stanton slack; 50 tons Swanwick slack; 50 wagons Manton Wood slack. (Notts/Derbyshire)
E. Foster & Co.	5 wagons Pleasley Top Hard (Notts)
Milner Thomas & Co.	50 tons Swanwick slack; 100 tons Eastwood hard locomotive coal. (Notts/Derbyshire)

Metropolitan K Class 2-6-4T stands alongside the coaling stage where, just to the left of the smokebox, can be discerned the 'S' on a Stephenson Clarke wagon. It would appear that the wagons were unloaded into the wicker baskets from which the bunkers were refilled. *Neil Parkhouse collection*

Taken at Quainton Road Station in 1935, a bucolic mixed train bound for Brill leaves behind 4-4-0T No. 41. The two Ricketts wagons are loaded with coal for a local gas works. *London Transport*

November 1914, painted red, lettered white with black shading.

September 1914, painted 'dark red', lettered white shaded black.

June 1915, painted red, lettered white with black shading.

September 1915, painted red, lettered white with black shading.

October 1914, painted red, lettered white with black shading.

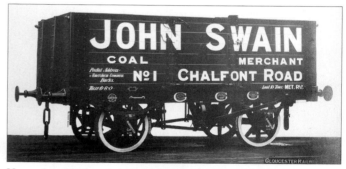

November 1914, painted red, lettered white with black shading.

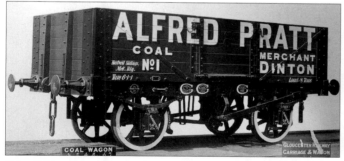

July 1914, painted red, lettered white with black shading.

The Metropolitan Railway, like all other railway companies, also registered coal wagons to run on its rails. No records appear to have survived, but a number of wagons registered to coal merchants on its rails were built by the Gloucester company and have been included for their rarity value. Interestingly, all are from the period 1914/15, were single wagon orders and many bear a very similar lettering layout suggestive of a co-operative purchase to obtain a better price or a successful Gloucester salesman. It is hoped to return to these wagons in a later volume with more details of their owners.

And finally two photographed in February 1915 and again painted red, lettered white with black shading. *all GRC&WCo.*

ERRATA

IN a similar manner to the photograph, *right*, text which is vital to the accuracy of, or to complement what has already been written in, a book such as this always seems to appear shortly after publication. The author can only write from what information is available at the time of writing and, despite cross checking of sources, there are instances where the records of wagon owners and even wagon builders are incorrect. That variations have been found between what should be impeccable and unquestionable primary sources, such as order books and minute books of wagon builders and owners, the *Colliery Guardian* Year Book and, in one instance, a Wagon Register, unfortunately leads to inaccuracies in a publication such as this. Occasionally reliance has to be placed on the memories of old miners, coalmen and railwaymen – now well into their eighties – which, although appear to be vivid, are becoming faded. If such sources are used, they are always recorded as such.

Therefore the following corrections to the content of *A First Collection* are willingly recorded with gratitude. In some instances additional information has been provided which is relevant to its contents.

Page 6: The Blidworth wagon was registered with the LMS, not the LNER. The registration numbers for these fifty wagons were 141083 to 141132. Further wagons built for the Newstead Colliery Company (p.86) between 1934 and 1937 were:

1901 - 2000	Central Wagon Co.	1934/5
2001 - 2100	Central Wagon Co.	1935/6
2101 - 2200	S. J. Claye	1934.
2201 - 2300	S. J. Claye	1935
2351 - 2400	Central Wagon Co.	1936
2401 - 2425	S. J. Claye	1936
2426 - 2475	S. J. Claye	1937
2476 - 2500	Wm Rigley	1936
2501 - 2550	Central Wagon Co.	1936

Page 27: The correct progression of mergers between the various companies controlled by Cammell Laird Ltd was that Cammell Laird and its various wagon building subsidiaries (including Midland of Birmingham) merged with Metropolitan to form the Metropolitan-Cammell company.

Pp.22-29: City of Birmingham Gas Department. Further photographic evidence suggests that the 75 wagons No's 1401 to 1475 were in fact originally lettered 'Gas Department' as were those No's 1801 to 1900 built by Pickering. The abbreviated form was, from photographs taken in the early 1920s, applied and standardised at the first repainting.

The 'missing numbers' between 2357 and 2606 were actually built for the Gas Department, although there are no records in any of its minutes that this was actually carried out. The 350 wagons ordered from Metro Cammell in the late 1930s were numbered 2916 to 3015 and 4501 to 4750. No wagons were built for the related Electric Supply Department.

Page 49: G. J. Cockerell, Ricketts and Rickett Smith were all eventually trading subsidiaries of the coal giant Wm Cory &

A late arrival which would have helped in the quest to establish the accuracy of the City of Birmingham Gas Dept. wagon lettering is this maker's photo of No. 1455, which shows the word 'Department' spelt out in full. Empty return is hard to read but appears to be Hardwick.

Sons. Other subsidiaries whose names are well known in the retail trade were Dinham Fawcus of London; Allen & Boggis of Sudbury and Mellonie & Goulder of Ipswich. Also trading subsidiaries of Wm. Cory & Sons, but operating on a larger scale, were Hull & Blyth Limited and Steamship Owners & Trading Co.

Page 57: These wagons were not of the standard RCH design.

Page 66: The wagon at the Kidderminster Railway Museum is not an original Highley wagon but came from the British Sugar Corporation. The Severn Valley line ran to Shrewsbury not Wellington.

Page 68: W. H. Kynaston commenced business in 1919. He was followed into the business by his son Rowland in 1937. The office moved to 13 Talbot Road, Fallowfield around 1950. The business was based at Mauldeth Road Station and a road vehicle was kept in a garage at the entrance to the sidings. The business survived until 1971. Although the colliery used is not recalled it is remembered that five or six wagons came into the sidings each delivery and that during the summer the coal was removed from the wagons and placed in a compound next to the garage so that the wagons could be released and avoid demurrage charges.

Page 91: The New Lount wagon of the Leicestershire Colliery & Pipe Co. is a new wagon, although the photograph certainly suggests otherwise. It is from an order for 100 wagons, No's 1250 to 1349, registered with the LMS (No's 155230 to 155329). Further wagons owned by this company additional to those described were No's 800 to 899, also built by the Central Wagon Company in 1927.

Page 118: The colliery has now been identified as the Lady Victoria Colliery, Newtongrange, Midlothian, the home of the Scottish Mining Museum.

ACKNOWLEDGEMENTS & SOURCES

AS in *Private Owner Wagons: A First Collection* the tally of sources from which the material contained herein is lengthy, almost as long as that volume. It is registered with considerable gratitude to all of the Archives and repositories listed below, as well as with grateful thanks to those individuals who have contributed to the contents of the present volume, and also those who have assisted the author with photographs, advice, encouragement, and who have pointed out errors which occurred in the first volume of this series. As before, at each of the institutions visited for the purpose of research the author was greeted cordially and enthusiastically assisted. In most instances it was amazing to see just how much interest a photograph of a Private Owner wagon generated within the county archives of its home base.

First and foremost thanks are overwhelmingly due to the staff of the Gloucestershire Record Office, custodians of the written and photographic records of the Gloucester Railway Carriage & Wagon Company. The agenda and minute books of the monthly directors meetings and the records of orders for new wagons, hires and sales of secondhand wagons, although not quite complete, together with 104 albums of photographs of the company's products taken over a period of over seventy years, are a unique and priceless record unequalled anywhere else in the country, and to Ian Pope, himself a distinguished author and publisher, for his assistance in procuring and reproducing what would have otherwise seemed unlikely photographs.

NATIONAL RAILWAY MUSEUM, YORK
Private Owner Wagon Registers, Great Central Railways, Great Eastern Railway, North Eastern Railway, Hull & Barnsley Railway, Southern Railway, LMS (incomplete) and LNER (incomplete): Order books of Charles Roberts Ltd, Wagon Builders.

PUBLIC RECORDS OFFICE, KEW
Private Owner Wagon Registers, Midland Railway, leading into the LMS, 1888 to 1927.

BIRMINGHAM CENTRAL LIBRARY ARCHIVES
Wagon order records and photographic records, (incomplete) Metropolitan-Cammell Wagon, Carriage & Finance Company, Midland & Metropolitan Amalgamated Carriage, Wagon & Finance Companies and their constituents.

STAFFORDSHIRE COUNTY RECORDS OFFICE, STAFFORD
Order books, delivery books, accounting records, The Birmingham Railway Carriage & Wagon Company: Various records, Nook and Wyrley Collieries, Cannock Old Coppice Colliery, Cannock Chase Colliery Co.: Coal contracts of City of Birmingham Electric Supply Department (included under miscellaneous papers of the Hamstead Colliery).

SHEFFIELD ARCHIVES
Letter Books (1924 to 1928) Hatfield Main Colliery Co.: Coal delivery book, (1913 to 1918) Bullcroft Colliery: 1950 *Colliery Directory*, published by The Colliery Guardian : 1945 *Colliery Directory*, published by H.M. Stationery Office: 1893 *Potts Mining Register*: Railway Rates book, circa 1920, of all sidings and stations, including all siding holders in the London area, (the latter is incomplete, all of the Great Northern sidings have been omitted): Markham Main Colliery: Sales records of the Kiveton Park Colliery.

NOTTINGHAMSHIRE ARCHIVES
Minute books of Nottingham Corporation Gas Dept: Accounts books of Nottingham and Clifton Collieries Ltd: Trading ledgers of New Hucknall, Blackwell and Shireoaks collieries: Wagon hire records, Clifton Colliery.

LONDON METROPOLITAN ARCHIVES
Minute books of the Uxbridge, Maidenhead, Wycombe and District Gas Co.: Minute books of the Metropolitan Railway.

NORTHAMPTONSHIRE ARCHIVES
Minute books of Wellingborough Gas Co.: correspondence and blueprints of Wagon Repairs Ltd, Wellingborough.

BERKSHIRE COUNTY RECORDS OFFICE, READING
Minute books of Reading Gas Company.

NATIONAL GRID TRANSCO plc, NATIONAL GAS ARCHIVES, WARRINGTON
Minute books of the following gas companies; Chester United, Burnley, Bingham, Melbourne and Northwich.

MANCHESTER CITY COUNCIL ARCHIVES AND LOCAL STUDY UNIT
Minute books of Manchester Corporation Gas Works.

GLAMORGAN COUNTY RECORDS OFFICE, CARDIFF
Trading records of Evans and Reid, coal factors, colliery agents and exporters: Trading records of Cardiff Steam Coal Collieries Ltd, Llanbradach: Minute books of Crynant Colliery Co.: Minute books of Duffryn Rhondda Colliery Co.: Wagon register, United National Collieries: Charter of amalgamation, Welsh Associated Collieries Ltd: *Cynon Coal* published by Cynon Historical Society: Production records, John Lancaster Steam Coal Collieries Ltd: *Directory of South Wales Collieries*, by Ray Lawrence (this otherwise unpublished record of the numerous collieries of South Wales is used as a standard reference, but in some instances it is considered unreliable as some dates do not agree with those in the Colliery Guardian year book).: Sales ledgers, Evans & Reid Coal Co.

ROTHERHAM METROPOLITAN ARCHIVES AND LOCAL STUDY CENTRE
Minute books and trading records, Wath Main Colliery Co. Ltd.

WEST YORKSHIRE ARCHIVES SERVICE, LEEDS
Trading records and correspondence books, Henry Briggs Ltd: Wagon fleet records, Nostell Colliery Co. Ltd.

SOUTHAMPTON ARCHIVES SERVICE, SOUTHAMPTON
Minute books of Southampton Corporation and electric supply department and Southampton Gas Light Co.

BRITISH LIBRARY, LONDON
Colliery Guardian Year Books, 1923 to 1940.

MERSEY MARITIME MUSEUM, LIVERPOOL
Lloyds register of shipping, various issues.
Minute books of Dinham Fawcus and Co; Hull and Blyth Ltd; Wm Cory and Sons; Steamship Owners Coal and Trading Co.
Shipping fleet details of Watts & Co and Elder Dempster Lines.
Minute books of Mersey Docks and Harbours Board.

LIVERPOOL CITY LIBRARY
Minute books of Liverpool Corporation Electricity Supply Dept.

NATIONAL MARITIME AND INDUSTRIAL MUSEUM OF WALES
Various items from photographic collection.

WARWICKSHIRE ARCHIVES
Coal contract and tender records, Warwickshire County Council.

CHESHIRE COUNTY COUNCIL, ARCHIVES AND LOCAL STUDIES
Various papers and trade journals which refer to the chemical industry of Cheshire, the formation of Imperial Chemical Industries, together with those of Brotherton and Co. Ltd.

HULL CITY LIBRARY, HULL
Hull as a Coal Port by H. E. C. Newnham.

For the supply of photographs, the Historical Model Railway Society, The Birmingham Central Library, the National Railway Museum, York, the Gloucestershire Records Office, Frank Ashley of Midrail Photographs, Michael Spick, Local Studies, Sheffield City Library, Audie Baker of the Kidderminster Railway Museum, Roger Carpenter, (including those from the Wakefield Collection), Allan C. Baker, Ian Pope, John Alsop, Bob Essery, Mark Smith, Neil Parkhouse, John Horne, Phil Coutanche and Colin Underwood.

Specific thanks are also due to Peter Bennett, curator of the photographic collection of the National Museums & Galleries of Wales at Nantgarw; Linda Danischewsky of Salt Union Limited for permission to reproduce photographs of their works; and to Bill Hudson.

For further information on the wagons of the City of Birmingham Gas Department, the Newstead Colliery and the New Lount Colliery Co., I am grateful to Mr John Horne. He has also kindly checked the manuscript for this volume and added to the text where relevant. To Colin Underwood for information relating to the various Franklins who were coal merchants in Bedfordshire and Hertfordshire and to Bill Kynaston for filling in the details of his family business. Finally to Ian Pope and Neil Parkhouse of Lightmoor Press for their help and encouragement.

MODELS

Throughout the text, references are made to models of the various wagons illustrated. As in *Private Owner Wagons: A First Collection*, these are identified by manufacturer and where a model is specially commissioned and sold only through a single dealer, this dealer is identified and their names and addresses are listed below.

Sherwood Models, 834 Mansfield Road, Daybrook, Nottingham NG5 3QF
Gee Dee Models, 21 Heathcote Street, Nottingham NG1 3AF
Geoffrey Allison, 90 Cheapside, Worksop, Notts S80 1HY
The Midlander, 393 Sheffield Road, Whittington Moor, Chesterfield S4 8LS
Rails of Sheffield, 27 Chesterfield Road, Sheffield S8 0RL
Holt Model Railways, Bishopston Road, Bishopston, Swansea.

MANUFACTURERS OF TRANSFERS, KITS AND SPECIAL COMMISSIONS
Powsides, Poplars Farm, Aythorpe Roding, Dunmow, Essex CM6 1RY
Osbornes Models, 2-4 Marcham Road, Abingdon, Oxon OX14 1AA.
Transfers of some Welsh wagons were and may still be available from Dragon Models, 9 Kingsley Close, Sully, CF64 5UW.

FURTHER READING

Thomas, A. G. *Modellers sketchbook of Private Owner Wagons*, No.1 Model Railways 1969.
Thomas, A. G. *Modellers sketchbook of Private Owner Wagons*, No. 2 Model Railways (undated).
Thomas, A. G. *Modellers sketchbook of Private Owner Wagons*, No. 3 Model Railways 1974.
Matthews, Peter. *Private Owner Wagons*, MAP Technical Publications, 1973.
Hudson, Bill. *Private Owner Wagons*, Vol. 1, Oxford Publishing Co. 1976.
Hudson, Bill. *Private Owner Wagons*, Vol. 2, Oxford Publishing Co. 1978.
Hudson, Bill. *Private Owner Wagons*, Vol. 3, Oxford Publishing Co. 1984.
Hudson, Bill. *Private Owner Wagons*, Vol. 4, Headstock Publications, 1987.
Montague, Keith. *Private Owner Wagons from the Gloucester Railway Carriage & Wagon Co. Ltd*, Oxford Publishing Co, 1981.
Tavender, L. *Coal Trade Wagons*, published privately, 1991.
Hudson, Bill. *Private Owner Wagons*, Oakwood Press, 1996.
Lloyd, Mike. *Private Owner Wagons on the Cambrian*, Welsh Railway Research Circle, 1998.
Watts, A.J. *Private Owner Wagons from the Ince Waggon and Ironworks*, HMRS, 1998.
Pope, Ian. *Private Owner Wagons of the Forest of Dean*, Lightmoor Press, 2002.
Turton, Keith. *Private Owner Wagons: A First Collection*, Lightmoor Press, 2003.
Johnson, Rob. *Modelling Aspects of the Coal Industry*, Book Law Publications, 2003